Proprio Italiano

Authentic Northern Italian Menus and Recipes

Proprio Italiano

Authentic Northern Italian Menus and Recipes

Lina Michi Coruccini

BETTERWAY PUBLICATIONS, INC.
WHITE HALL, VIRGINIA

Published by Betterway Publications, Inc.
P.O. Box 219
Crozet, VA 22932
(804) 823-5661

Cover design by Rick Britton
Cover photographs by Tom Vano
Photographs by Frank Spadarella and Gianni Limonta
Typography by Park Lane Associates

Library of Congress Cataloging-in-Publication Data

Corucinni, Lina Michi
    Proprio Italiano : authentic northern Italian menus and recipes /
Lina Michi Corucinni.
        p. cm.
    Includes index.
    ISBN 1-55870-221-0 (pbk.) : $14.95
    1. Cookery, Italian--Northern style. 2. Menus. I. Title.
TX723.2.N65C67 1991
641.5945--dc20   91-19480
                                                              CIP

Printed in the United States of America
0 9 8 7 6 5 4 3 2 1

I dedicate this book to my husband Roberto
for his love, his support, and his understanding.
He has given me the courage and strength to work
and write this book. Thank you so very much!

Acknowledgments

To all my friends who have encouraged and helped me in writing this book, I give my thanks and appreciation for all of your support.

I would like to express my appreciation to Frank Spadarella, Gianni Limonta, and Foto Pluto Figli who photographed all the Italian scenes and portraits in the book. To Tom Vano my many thanks for his beautiful food photography and to Biordi Art Imports of San Francisco for the use of their lovely Italian pottery and accessories in the photographs.

I also want to give my thanks and gratitude to a special person who has guided and advised me throughout this whole book project. My thanks go to Hilde Lee, who is not only my editor, but who has become a very good friend.

Contents

Introduction

I was born in Northern Italy in a small town near Lucca in the Tuscany region, where the soil is very rich, producing great wine and one of the best olive oils in the world. My fondest memories of my life in Italy were of family and friends gathering around the kitchen table, where the meal became a celebration of food and traditions. I missed that feeling of warmth and companionship when I came to America as a teenager fleeing the ravages of the Second World War.

I have always loved to be in the kitchen and to cook, because I love to eat. As a child I helped my mother with her cooking whenever I was not in school. Even today, cooking is a joy for me. In the winter months when it is cold and raining, I spend the whole day cooking and inventing new recipes. I love the smell, the aroma of the food, but most important, I love to watch my family and friends enjoy it with lots of enthusiasm and gusto. That is my reward and enjoyment.

I was encouraged by many people to write this book because they wanted my recipes. At first I did not know if I could put my cooking on paper, because I did not measure anything when I cooked. It was a pinch here and a little bit of that there. That is how I learned to cook from my mother. She was a great cook but usually prepared simple dishes. There were not many, but as she would say, it is not how many dishes you serve but how well each one is prepared. We could not afford fancy cuts of meat or fancy eating, but what we ate was fresh, seasoned well, and tasty.

There were also many Italian peasant dishes that were made at the time of my great-grandmother. The family was very poor and had gone through the war. Those so-called peasant dishes are still being served in restaurants today and are very popular for home entertaining. I have included some of these dishes in this book.

I return to Italy each year and visit with friends and relatives, including two cousins who have restaurants near Milan. I always pick up tips from them and new food ideas, which I have tried to incorporate in this book. It is a mixture of the old and new cuisine of northern Italy.

In Italy cooking is an art. The essence of the food is the perfect blending of ingredients, with sauces, spices, and herbs playing important roles. For example, the famous Tuscan olive oil is used in cooking, but sparingly. The Italians are known for their use of rice, pasta, beans, poultry, and, of course, veal. They are fond of game birds, particularly when roasted and accompanied by polenta.

The northern region of Italy is known for its rice dishes, its game dishes, and its delicious desserts and fried pastries. The delicate panettone yeast cake originated in the area and is used for celebrations in Italian homes.

The success of any meal, Italian or otherwise, depends not only on the preparation of the food but on the composition of the menu. Every dish on a menu should complement the others. The menu should also take advantage of available seasonal ingredients as well as the prevailing climate.

In Italy shopping for food is a daily routine. The food is chosen with great care. Cooking is very important, but so is the serving of the meal. In an Italian meal, the portions are small, but they are expected to be very good.

In the typical Italian meal, pasta, rice, or soup is served as a first course. Meat or fish will follow, accompanied by vegetables, and then a very simple salad is served with an oil and vinegar or lemon juice dressing. This may be followed by a cheese of the area. Fruit and/or dessert end the meal with coffee or espresso. Wine is usually served as an accompaniment to the meal.

Keeping in mind the traditional dishes of northern Italy, the seasonal preferences, and the availability of ingredients, I have tried to create Italian menus to suit American occasions. Some of the American events do not occur in Italy, but I have created a typical menu for them. I have focused on readily available ingredients, even though some of them may be seasonal.

In northern Italy, as in the regions of the United States, there is no longer a distinct division of cuisines. Travel and easy transportation facilities have melded much of the Italian cuisine into one and have also brought foreign ingredients into this cuisine. For example, salmon, once thought to be only a northern European ingredient, is now almost an everyday item in northern Italian cooking. The world has gotten smaller, and the once exotic and foreign ingredients are almost regarded as "our own."

For your convenience I have also included a preparation guide with each menu to enable you to schedule much of the cooking before the meals are to be served. Bon Appetito!

I.

The Makings of an Italian Meal

The Typical Italian Meal

The typical Italian meal consists of various courses. Some meals may only have two courses—the entrée and a salad or dessert—others may include five courses. The salad is often regarded as the main part of the meal, and cheese and fruit may be an interlude before a sweet dessert. Following are the courses in the order they are served. There is also a small description of each course.

Antipasto
Appetizer

Il Primo
First Course

Il Secondo
Main Course

La Verdura
Vegetables

Il Formaggio
Cheese

La Frutta e il Dolce
Fruit and Dessert

Caffè
Coffee

Antipasto—Appetizer

The word *antipasto* means the course that is eaten before the meal begins. It literally means "before the pasta" since pasta is often served as a first course. The antipasto is supposed to stimulate the appetite and can be served either cold or hot. Antipasto varies from region to region, and many antipasto dishes could be eaten as a main course.

The quantities of antipasto dishes should be small, since they are supposed to stimulate the appetite, not satisfy it. Appetizers are selected to complement the meal and not overpower it.

Il Primo—First Course

Often a plate of pasta or risotto is served as the first course. Many wonderful soups also are served as a first course—fish, vegetable, or bean soup. A northern Italian dish that is served as a first course is polenta, either fried or baked. It is served with simple sauces and often accompanies meat or poultry dishes.

Il Secondo—Main Course

The main course consists of meat, game, poultry, or fish dishes. The meat and fish are prepared in many different ways — roasted, stew, grilled, or fried. For special meals, two or three main dishes are served.

La Verdura—Vegetables

Vegetables are very important in Italy and must always be very fresh. Usually the vegetables that are served are the ones in season at the time. Italian salads are made of mixtures of cultivated and wild plants. They may contain many different types of leaves and are served with a simple dressing.

Il Formaggio—Cheese

After the main course, cheese is often served. Many different kinds of cheese are made in Italy with many regional variations. In northern Italy the most famous cheeses are: Parmigiano Reggiano (Parmesan cheese); pecorino, which is a more rustic cheese; Gorgonzola, a creamy blue cheese; and fontina, which is semi-soft and used for cooking and for fondue.

La Frutta e il Dolce—Fruit and Dessert

Fresh fruit of the season is always served after a meal. Special desserts usually are served for special occasions, such as anniversaries, birthdays, and Christmas and Easter dinners. Some of the fruit-based desserts are fruit tarts and pies, fruit sorbets, and ice creams. Sweets and cakes are usually served at holiday dinners, for example, Panettone, Panforte, and Colomba cake.

Caffè—Coffee

Coffee is always served in Italy at the end of a meal, and it is always served black. The Italian coffee is called *espresso*, and it is served in small cups. Italians drink it anytime during the day, not just after a meal. In the morning they drink what is called *cappuccino*. This is an espresso coffee with whipped milk on top, and it is served in a larger cup. Coffee is also used in Italy as an ingredient in many different kinds of desserts.

SOME UNIQUE ASPECTS OF ITALIAN CUISINE

Each country and region has its own unique dishes and methods of food preparation. Also each cook has his or her own preferences for methods of shopping, styles of cooking, and presentation of the food. I am no exception, and I want to share with you some of my thoughts and ideas on various aspects of an Italian meal.

Soup

Homemade broth is an indispensable ingredient of good Italian cooking. I prepare big batches of it, which I freeze in plastic containers. I also keep odd chicken parts and beef bones in the freezer and add them to the pot when I make broth. Bones are as useful as meat because they give body as well as flavor.

Soup is often the first course in an Italian meal, and it is frequently served once a day in Italy, mostly in the evening because it is very light. I have great childhood memories of my mother in the kitchen preparing our Sunday dinner. Sunday was the day that we would invite friends for dinner, and she would prepare a beef soup as a first course. Our house was filled with the aroma of the broth simmering. Her soup would give a glow to our cheeks.

If you are making the soup because you want to eat the boiled meat or chicken, then put the meat in water that is boiling. The boiling water seals in the flavor similar to the way browning meat does. If you want to make a rich broth to use for cooking, then you place all the ingredients, meat bones, and vegetables covered by cold water in a stock pot. Cooking in cold water takes away the flavors of the ingredients, while boiling water seals them in.

Bread

The Italians are said to eat more bread than any other nationality. They cannot eat without it, and it has to be fresh, baked the same day. Stale bread is fed to the animals.

The bread that the Italians eat is white. Some of it is thick, and country bread is very coarse. Each region makes their own style of bread. I love "il Panino" (the bun); it is pure white and has to be eaten the same day it is baked. The inside of the bun is almost empty; there is very little dough.

There are some very good recipes created for using stale bread. In the summer I make panzanella, which is stale bread with fresh vegetables, and in the winter I make zuppa di fagioli, with stale bread cooked in a bean broth, with the addition of Parmesan cheese. Many Italian recipes use bread as a base. Fried bread in olive oil is a base for filet mignon or roasted quails. Slices of bread and crumbs are used for stuffing meat, chicken, fowl, fish, and vegetables. Italians also make a bread cake from leftover bread and candied fruit. Toasted bread slices are often rubbed with garlic and sprinkled with olive oil.

Fritatta

One of the most common Italian dishes is the fritatta. This is an open-face Italian omelet. The most common one is made with zucchini, but other vegetables, ham, sausage, cheese, and herbs can also be used.

A fritatta is usually cooked in a heavy skillet over low heat on top of the stove, but it can also be cooked in the oven. I prefer to cook mine on top of the stove and then finish it under the broiler. The preparation of a fritatta is very simple.

When serving, slice the fritatta in wedges like a pie. It may be served hot or cold, for lunch, as a main course, or as a vegetable accompaniment.

Risotto

The basic method of making a risotto in Italy is as follows: The rice must first be sautéed in butter and oil or just butter, usually with onion but sometimes with other vegetables. The simmering broth is added a little at a time, and additional broth is added only when the rice has absorbed the liquid that was added before. The rice is cooked at an even heat, not too high, not too low. At the end, more butter and some Parmesan cheese are always added. The risotto is left a few minutes, then stirred, transferred to a dish, and eaten as soon as it is ready.

You will notice that in my risotto recipes I cook the rice with the entire broth, covered, over low heat for 15 minutes, or until the rice is cooked through but still firm to the bite. I find this method works perfectly. The grains separate, yet they are bound together in a creamy consistency. This method leaves time to prepare other dishes while getting the same results as the basic method.

Vegetables

You will notice as you read the recipes in this book that vegetables, probably even more than pasta, are the main base of Italian cooking. Vegetables are mixed with rice or pasta, used as appetizers, in soups, and in elaborate main dishes. They are also used in between courses as a palate cleanser instead of a salad.

In Italy, the vegetables are always served on their own separate plate just like pasta or rice dishes. In summer, when it gets very hot, the Italians live almost entirely on fresh vegetables. They are prepared in many ways, but are frequently very simply dressed with olive oil and lemon juice. Italians also love raw vegetables dipped in olive oil, pepper, and salt. Even today some of the best restaurants serve vegetables this way, and this is called "Pinzimonio."

One of the extraordinary sights that I love when I go to Italy is an Italian open market full of vegetable stalls. This is called "mercato." There you find colorful mounds of vegetables and fruit picked fresh that morning on the farm. The Italian housewife inspects all this abundance for a while. She touches, she smells, she compares from one stall to another, and sometimes she also bargains.

Salads

In Italy salads are never served as a first course. They are always served after the main course, since they are supposed to clean and refresh the palate before the cheese, fruit, or dessert is served.

When serving a salad after a very special or heavy meal, it should be a light and simple one. A salad made with mixed cooked vegetables and cheese or eggs is perfect for lunch.

Italian salad dressings are very simple but tasty. They consist of olive oil, salt, and wine vinegar. The olive oil should be a fruity one and used generously. However, be stingy with the vinegar since too much can ruin a salad. Black pepper can be added and should always be ground fresh. Lemon juice may be substituted for the vinegar and is quite nice for summer salads.

Desserts

In Italy the pastry shops provide most of the sweets and desserts. The desserts that are prepared at home are very simple. Fresh fruit in season is usually served with a platter of different cheeses.

Most Italians would rather miss dessert than a first course, and I am one of them. I would rather have fruit anytime than a fancy dessert. When a dessert is served at home, it is on a special occasion or on holidays. Pastries are sometimes served in the afternoon with espresso coffee. However, Italians prefer to go out to have coffee and pastry.

II.

Stocking Your Pantry with Italian Ingredients

The Italian Pantry

The following are some of the ingredients that you might want to have in your pantry for cooking Italian food:

Italian Arborio rice to make risotto or to use in soups.

A few of your favorite dried pastas, so that you will have a variety to pair with different sauces.

Cornmeal for making polenta—I keep two kinds. I have the coarse cornmeal that needs to cook for 45 minutes and be stirred constantly, and I have the instant 5-minute polenta for when I decide at the last minute that I want to serve polenta.

Dried white beans (cannellini), lentils, and chickpeas.

Canned goods including Italian peeled tomatoes and tomato paste. You may also want cans of cannellini, garbanzo, and kidney beans. Cans of tuna for salads and of anchovy fillets to add additional flavors to various dishes should also be available. There are green and black olives, plenty of bottles of extra virgin olive oil, red wine vinegar, balsamic vinegar, and a jar each of capers and peppercorns.

Packages of dried porcini mushrooms are a good idea since they keep for a long time. I also keep saffron for risotto, soups, and meat dishes.

A wedge of Parmesan cheese is an essential ingredient for Italian cooking, and it should be stored in the refrigerator, tightly wrapped in aluminum foil. It should be grated fresh as needed. Both mozzarella and fontina cheese are good to have on hand, and they must be kept in the refrigerator.

Other refrigerator items include a tube each of anchovy paste, garlic paste, and tomato paste. The tubes are better to use and not wasteful. Pesto sauce in a jar or plastic container for pasta or to add to sauces, soups, or to spread over bread should also be kept in the refrigerator. I usually buy a large whole piece of pancetta (Italian bacon), keep it in the refrigerator, and slice it when needed. Also I buy a thick chunk of prosciutto and cut it when needed.

Almonds, pine nuts, and walnuts should be kept in the freezer because they will remain fresh longer than if stored in the refrigerator. In my freezer, I also have homemade chicken and beef stock, as well as vegetable stock for risotto, sauces, and soups. My freezer also contains some Italian sausages.

Espresso coffee should be stored in a tight glass jar or you can buy the espresso beans and grind fresh as needed.

BASIC INGREDIENTS
FOR ITALIAN COOKING

This list of basic ingredients for Italian cooking will help acquaint you with many of the ingredients used in the recipes in this book. It is always a good idea to use only the freshest ingredients available; choose only the finest and prepare them with care.

Beans

In Italy cranberry beans and cannellini beans are grown in the summer and eaten fresh at that time. The rest of the year dried ones are used, particularly in soups such as minestrone and pasta e fagioli. They are also very tasty boiled, drained, and seasoned with olive oil, salt, and pepper. Beans are combined with tuna in a salad and with tomato sauce for a side dish.

Cheeses

Italy produces many wonderful cheeses. Try to buy imported cheese, since the domestic imitations do not always match the taste and style of the Italian original. Some of the best known cheeses used in this book are as follows:
Parmesan cheese comes from the Parma region and from Reggio Emilia. It is made from cow's milk and aged for two or three years. The drier outer part of the cheese is best for grating. The inside part, if it is still soft, is better for eating.
Always grate Parmesan cheese fresh when needed in a recipe.

Store it tightly wrapped in the refrigerator. Parmesan cheese is used in sauces, with pasta, soup, meat, salad, and bread. This cheese is excellent cut in chunks and eaten with a glass of Italian wine.

Pecorino is a cheese made from sheep's milk. When aged for a few months, it is eaten as a snack or as a dessert. When aged longer, it is used for grating.

The Italian pecorino for grating that is more familiar in this country is the Romano, which is from the Rome area. Romano cheese has a sharper flavor than Parmesan cheese. Sometimes the two cheeses are used together. Romano cheese is an excellent combination with pesto sauce.

Fontina cheese, which is made from cow's milk, is a soft cheese with a delicate nutty flavor. It is eaten plain with bread or fruit or is used in chicken and veal dishes.

Gorgonzola is a very delicate blue-veined cheese. It is used in salads or just eaten by itself.

Mozzarella is made from cow's milk and is the basic pizza cheese, but it is also used in many other dishes. In Italy, an old-fashioned genuine mozzarella is made from water buffalo's milk and is served fresh. Hardened mozzarella is found in specialty Italian shops.

The best Italian ricotta is dry and made from sheep's or water buffalo's milk. Ricotta sold in this country most often is made from whole milk and is not as perishable as true ricotta. Ricotta is used in many desserts.

Provolone is the cheese that you see always hanging in Italian stores and in pictures of Italian markets. It is a firm cheese with a smoky flavor.

Mascarpone is a rich, fresh cheese that is often used in desserts and pastries instead of whipped cream.

Cold Cuts

Also called Parma ham, prosciutto is one of the most common foods in the Italian diet. It comes raw or cooked. Prosciutto is salted and air-dried fresh ham. The seasoning and aging process cures the ham completely, a process that takes many months.

Prosciutto varies in flavor depending on the region of its origin. Some are more salty and some sweet. In some regions it is smoked, which is very unusual. When a recipe calls for prosciutto, it refers to the uncooked ham. It should always be cut paper thin.

Bresaola originated in the region of Lombardy. It has now become a favorite appetizer all over Italy. Salted, air-dried, and pressed, it may be made from different cuts of beef. You can serve it very simply, sliced like prosciutto and with a little lemon juice and oil, or in sauces for pasta with butter, cream, and herbs. Bresaola can be compared with the German Bündnerfleisch or the Swiss Viande de Grisons.

The best mortadella is made in Italy in Bologna. Mortadella is made from finely ground pure pork and is flavored with wine. Sometimes pistachio nuts are added, as well as large white cubes of fat.

Sausages come in two versions—mild or spiced. They are made with ground pork and pancetta. Some domestic sausages are seasoned with fennel seeds.

Pancetta is Italian bacon. It is not smoked but is cured with salt and spices. Sliced thin, it is great eaten with French bread as a cold cut. It is used to flavor dishes and for pasta sauces.

Olive Oil

Olive oil is an essential ingredient in Italian cuisine. It is used for browning, braising, and broiling; in soups, stews, risottos, frittatas, and pastas. Olive oil is the dressing for salads and the condiment for antipasto dishes. It is also the finishing touch for vegetables.

The very best olive oil is extra virgin oil, which is obtained from the first cold pressing of the finest, hand-picked olives. Green or green-gold, it is aromatic and tastes mellow and nutty with no bitter aftertaste. The second best grade of olive oil is virgin. It is obtained through continuing pressing of the olives and is aromatic, green, and flavorful. Pure olive oil is the last grade produced for general use and the kind most imported in this country. The word pure means nothing more than that the oil came only from olives. It is pale yellow and has only a slight olive aroma and taste.

Tomato Paste

Tomato paste is not a substitute for tomatoes, but sometimes one teaspoon or tablespoon of tomato paste adds special zest to a dish. The Italian imported brands are packaged in tubes so that you can use a little at a time and not waste what is left.

HERBS, SPICES, AND
OTHER FLAVOR ENHANCERS

There is a world of a difference between the taste of fresh herbs and that of dried ones. Fresh herbs can either be grown in a little garden plot or on the kitchen window sill. They can also be purchased at many supermarkets.

Since I have a vegetable garden, I always grow rosemary, sage, oregano, basil, thyme, and mint. I also have Italian parsley and regular parsley. Growing your own herbs gives you the opportunity to freeze or dry the excess.

In some of the recipes I use the term "dry Italian seasoning." One tablespoon of dry Italian seasoning contains thyme, basil, rosemary, savory, sage, marjoram, and oregano. One tablespoon of this seasoning is approximately equivalent to 3 teaspoons: ½ teaspoon each of dried thyme, basil, oregano, and rosemary and ¼ teaspoon each dried savory, sage, and marjoram. If fresh herbs are not available, you can substitute dried ones. Remember to store the dried herbs in a dark, dry place and discard them once a year or if they start to smell musty and begin to lose their potency.

The following is a brief description of some of the herbs and spices used in this book:

BAY LEAVES: The bay leaf is a sweet, aromatic herb native to the Mediterranean area. Dried or fresh, whole or chopped, it is used with fish and meats.

BASIL: Basil is more pungent fresh, as when dried it loses much of its smell. However, basil freezes well. To freeze basil, rinse the leaves, pat them dry, then freeze in plastic bags. Chop while they are still frozen and add them to cooked dishes. You can also place chopped basil in a glass jar with olive oil, cover tightly, and freeze the mixture. Basil is a natural companion of tomatoes.

BLACK PEPPER: Black pepper should always be freshly ground with a pepper mill. There are five different kinds of peppercorns —white, black, red, green, and rose—and they are used either whole or ground.

GARLIC: The fresher the garlic is, the more subtle the flavor. Garlic is essential to Italian cooking. It is used whole, crushed, minced, slit, or chopped in many recipes. Garlic should be stored in a cool, dry place. You may keep peeled garlic in a jar covered with olive oil in the refrigerator. However, do not store it for a long period of time because it will lose some of its strength.

MARJORAM and OREGANO: Marjoram and oregano are related plants. Marjoram is sweet and has a more delicate flavor than oregano. It is often used with other herbs in meat dishes. Marjoram is used more in Northern Italy, while oregano is rarely used. Oregano is used in pizza, seafood dishes, and spaghetti sauces in Southern Italy.

MINT: Mint is the herb of the early Romans. Although used in fruit drinks and with poultry and fish, mint is primarily used in this book as a garnish and with marinated fruits.

NUTMEG: Nutmeg is used in egg dishes and white sauces and with some vegetables. It is also used as a spice in baking.

PARSLEY: Parsley can be used for flavoring or as a garnish. The Italian parsley has a flatter leaf and a greater aroma than the curly-leafed parsley. Both are available fresh in supermarkets throughout the year.

ROSEMARY: Rosemary thrives in the sea air and heat of the Mediterranean, but it also grows well in other climates. It is traditionally used with meat dishes, primarily lamb, poultry, and also some seafood.

SAFFRON: Saffron is a spice used primarily in risottos. It has its own characteristic flavor and turns brilliant yellow when mixed with food. Saffron is also used in fish soups and chicken dishes.

SAGE: Sage is a great flavor enhancer for poultry, veal, and roasted potatoes. Sage is also used with wild game, especially small birds like doves, quails, and pigeons.

THYME: When using fresh thyme, use only the leaves. Whole leaves, fresh or dried, are excellent with seafood, cheese dishes, eggs, meats, soups, and Mediterranean vegetables such as eggplant and zucchini.

In addition to herbs and spices the following also add flavoring to Italian cooking:

LEMON: Lemon has a distinctive perfume and flavor in both its juice and peel. It adds a piquancy to almost any type of food, including meat, chicken, fish, fruit, and vegetables.

MUSHROOMS: Porcini are the most popular wild mushrooms in Italian cooking, but other types are also used. The cultivated mushrooms are primarily eaten raw in a salad. Fresh or dried mushrooms are used as seasonings in sauces, risottos, pastas, omelettes, and soups. When dried mushrooms are used in Italian cooking, it is always the porcini because of their special aroma. To reconstitute them, porcini mushrooms should be soaked in warm water for 20 minutes to half an hour and then rinsed to wash away any dirt that might still cling to them. The soaking liquid should be strained through a very fine sieve and can be used in soups and sauces.

ONIONS: There are many different kinds of onions. Yellow onions are used for frying and sautéeing; in soups and sauces; and in meat, fish, poultry, wild game, and vegetable dishes. The red onions are used raw for green salads, with sliced tomatoes, white beans, raw meat, and tuna, salmon, or chicken salads.

TOMATOES: Although fresh tomatoes are always preferred for salads, canned Italian plum tomatoes are frequently used in cooking. They are firm and fleshy and have good flavor.

PASTA AND RICE

Which is better, fresh pasta or dried pasta? This is an impossible question to answer, because only you can decide which of the two you prefer. There are many good brands of dried pastas from which to choose on the shelves of the supermarkets. Fresh pasta is usually sold in the dairy case.

Italians prefer dried pasta, as do I. It gives me better control when cooking, and I like the consistency better. I prefer to spend my time making a good sauce instead of making a fresh pasta by hand or by machine.

The cooking time for pasta depends on whether it is dried or fresh. In either case, the pasta should be cooked *al dente* or "to the tooth." Fresh pasta usually takes 2 to 3 minutes to cook. As soon that is done, pour a glass of cold water into the pot before you drain it. This will immediately stop the cooking action and prevent the pasta from becoming mushy. Dried pasta will take 8 to 10 minutes to cook for most types. When boiling the pasta, make sure you are using a large saucepan with large amounts of water. Add one teaspoon of salt per quart and always bring the water to a high boil before adding the pasta. Drain the pasta after it has finished cooking.

After the pasta has drained, add it to the pan in which the sauce is being cooked, mix, and let the pasta absorb the sauce and cook for a few minutes. Another method is to place the drained pasta in a heated dish, add the hot sauce, and then mix. Serve with freshly grated Parmesan cheese. If the pasta has to sit for a while before adding the sauce, toss it with some butter or oil, otherwise the pasta will stick together.

There are different ways of serving pasta. A plain or stuffed pasta can be served with different sauces or it may be cooked in broth.

Pasta cooked in the oven is baked in layers in a sauce, and pasta can be part of a frittata. Pasta is also used to make different kinds of pasta salads.

There are so many different pasta names and shapes that even Italians sometimes get confused, because in different regions they are called by different names. Pasta comes in different forms, sizes, thicknesses, textures, and colors. It may be long and narrow, short and broad, smooth or ridged, solid or hollow. Different pastas require different sauces.

I have used some of the more popular shaped pastas for the sauces in this book. They are:

FETTUCCINE: The Roman version of tagliatelle but a little narrower and a little thicker than Bolognese tagliatelle. Fettuccine is served with cream sauces, with butter and rosemary, and with other sauces.

FUSILLI: Also known as tortiglioni or rotelle. The fusilli are large tubular pasta shaped like a corkscrew. They are ideally sauced with a thick stew, creamy sauces with meat, or with vegetables such as zucchini and bell peppers.

LASAGNE: Lasagne is traditional in many regions of Italy. Each area makes a different dough, which is cut in different lengths and widths and used with a variety of sauces and stuffings. The best lasagne is made only with flour and eggs and is the traditional dough of the Emilia-Romagna region. In that region lasagne is a green dough made with chopped spinach and layered with a meat sauce and béchamel sauce (white sauce).

LINGUINE: Linguine is a long, flat pasta, narrow and slightly tapering at the edges, about $1/8$ inch wide. Linguine can be used instead of spaghetti or tagliolini.

MACHERONCINI: These are small, short, narrow, hollow macaroni that come either ridged or smooth. They can be served with a variety of sauces and are used in a pasta salad or pasta pie.

PAGLIA E FIENO: This means straw and hay. It is a pasta consisting of yellow and green noodles. The green noodles are made with spinach, and the yellow noodles are made with egg.

PAPPARDELLE: Pappardelle is a wide egg noodle, about ¾ inch wide, cut with a fluted pastry wheel. Pappardelle is one of the traditional pastas from Tuscany, which is served during the hunting season with a sauce of wild hare.

PENNE RIGATE OR PENNE LISCIE: Penne come either ridged or smooth. They are cut diagonally at both ends, which are shaped like a quill pen. Penne are served with rich sauces, but are just as tasty served with a simple basil and tomato sauce.

TAGLIATELLE: The classic egg noodles of Emilia-Romagna, and a specialty of Bologna. Tagliatelle are made with dough of flour and egg, rolled out thin, and then cut into thin strips ¼ inch wide.

TORTELLINI: Tortellini are also known as cappelletti in Romagna. The best known tortellini are from Bologna. They are small round dumplings shaped like a ring and stuffed with meat. Tortellini are traditionally served in hot broth to which Parmesan cheese has been added. Different stuffings are also used for tortellini, and they can be served with butter, cream, and Parmesan cheese as well as other sauces.

RICE: Italy's primary rice-growing region is the Po Valley where four types of rice are grown, ranging from short to long grain rice. The best and the most exported variety of Italian rice is Arborio. This rice is ideal for preparing risotto because it absorbs a lot of liquid while cooking and swells up without breaking apart.

Rice can also be served boiled and mixed simply with butter and Parmesan cheese or in a salad with tuna, grilled bell pepper, tomatoes, and a few anchovies. It is used mainly in soups and stuffings, as well as for croquettes, fritters, and baked rice molds.

CONCERNING RAW EGGS

There is growing concern about the threat of salmonella contamination of raw eggs. While only six cases of salmonella were reported from January to May of 1991, and none has been traced to eggs, the following recommendations should be made:

The very young, the very old, and the chronically ill should not consume anything containing raw egg.

Check eggs for broken shells and discard any found.

Refrigerate eggs as soon after purchase as possible.

Dishes containing raw egg should be consumed immediately.

Freezing dishes containing raw egg in a 0° freezer keeps the bacteria from growing.

Items containing raw egg should be kept at room temperature only as long as it takes to prepare them.

III.

Menus and Recipes

Seasonal Menus

Una Festa di Primavera
A Spring Feast

Una Cena d'Estate alla Brace
A Summer Barbecue

Una Serata in Autunno
An Evening in Autumn

Invito di Minestre d'Inverno
Invitation to Winter Soups

Una Festa di Primavera
A Spring Feast

Risotto Primavera
Risotto with Spring Vegetables

Petto di Vitello Ripieno
Stuffed Breast of Veal

Patate con Funghi al Forno
Baked Potatoes with Mushrooms

Asparagi Saltati
Sautéed Asparagus

Torta di Zabaglione
Zabaglione Cake

Caffè
Coffee

SERVES 10

Spring is the time when the first flowers bloom, trees leaf out, birds are back singing, and lovers stroll in the park. Spring is also evident in the produce markets, which display tender young vegetables. I chose this menu to take advantage of the new vegetables in the market, especially the peas and the asparagus.

The risotto, which is prepared with spring vegetables, is a very light dish. If fresh peas are not available in your area, thawed frozen ones may be substituted. Since the dish is a delicate one, I recommend using homemade broth for this risotto. Canned broth is too strong. Avoid overcooking the vegetables for the risotto because overcooking will alter the texture and crispness of the vegetables.

The breast of veal makes a beautiful, colorful, and elegant presentation, as well as being very tasty. The accompanying potato and porcini mushroom casserole is from the Liguria region of Italy. It has an unusual flavor combination because the potatoes absorb the flavors of the porcini mushrooms and the Parmesan cheese. Crisply sautéed asparagus provides a refreshing interlude between the main course and dessert.

The meal ends with the cooling zabaglione dessert, which has a rich and creamy taste. Topped with the fresh strawberries, it is a great spring dessert.

Preparations

All the vegetables for the risotto may be cut and cleaned early in the day and stored in the refrigerator. Cook the vegetables just before your company arrives and set them aside. Fifteen minutes before dinner, cook the rice, reheat the vegetables, and assemble the risotto.

The stuffing for the veal pocket may be prepared the day before. Place it in a covered bowl and refrigerate it. The day of the party, stuff the veal pocket, sew it, and place the veal in a roasting pan. If it fits your schedule, the veal may be cooked to finish 2 hours before dinner and kept warm. Or, you may desire to cook the veal so that it will be done just before you serve the entrée.

The potato and mushroom casserole should be prepared about an hour before your guests arrive. It may be covered and set aside for a short while. Place the casserole in the oven one hour before dinner.

Much of the asparagus preparation may be done in the afternoon. Clean and cut the asparagus and onions and cook them for only 10 minutes of the cooking time. The asparagus will stay crisper if it is not seasoned at this time. Remove the asparagus from the heat and keep it at room temperature. That evening, finish cooking the asparagus 15 minutes before you serve the meal, adding the seasonings and the cheese. The cooking time may seem lengthy, but this is due to the large amount of asparagus in the recipe. If using very tender, small stalks of asparagus, you may want to decrease the cooking time by about 5 minutes. The asparagus will remain warm while dinner is in progress.

Since the Zabaglione Cake freezes well, it can be made anytime during the week previous to the dinner. However, if you prefer not to freeze the cake, it can be prepared the day before and refrigerated. The strawberries may be cleaned the day before and arranged on top of the cake just before the party.

~ Risotto Primavera ~
Risotto with Spring Vegetables

6½ cups homemade chicken broth
6 tablespoons (¾ stick) unsalted
   butter
2 tablespoons olive oil
½ cup chopped pancetta
1 cup diced carrot
2 medium leeks, sliced thin
1 cup sliced celery
1 cup coarsely chopped zucchini
1 cup fresh peas (or thawed frozen
   peas)
1 cup fresh small asparagus pieces

½ teaspoon salt
½ teaspoon freshly ground black
   pepper
3 cups Italian Arborio rice
2 large fresh ripe tomatoes or 2
   large canned tomatoes, peeled,
   seeded, and diced
½ cup freshly grated Parmesan
   cheese
2 tablespoons chopped fresh parsley
Additional grated Parmesan cheese

Place the chicken broth in a large saucepan and keep it barely simmering.

Melt 4 tablespoons of the butter with the olive oil in a heavy deep frying pan. Add the pancetta and sauté over medium high heat for few minutes. Then add the carrots, leeks, celery, zucchini, and fresh peas. (If using frozen peas, add them with the asparagus later.) Add ½ cup of the simmering broth and continue cooking.

When the vegetables are half cooked, add the asparagus (and the frozen peas, if used). Season with salt and pepper and simmer until the vegetables are barely tender.

Bring the remaining 6 cups of chicken broth to a fast boil. Add rice, stir, and bring to a boil again. Cover and cook on low heat for 15 minutes. While the rice is cooking, add the diced tomatoes to the vegetables, mix well, and continue cooking the vegetables very slowly until the rice is done. The rice should be tender and cooked through, but firm to the bite.

Combine the cooked rice with the vegetables, and add the remaining butter and the grated Parmesan cheese. Stir gently but thoroughly. Sprinkle the risotto with chopped parsley. Serve immediately on individual plates or from a large heated platter, with additional grated Parmesan cheese.

SERVES 10

~ *Petto di Vitello Ripieno* ~
Stuffed Breast of Veal

Breast of veal with bone-in, 10 to
    12 ribs, with a pocket cut into
    the meat for stuffing
3 slices white bread, crusts removed
1/3 cup milk
1/4 pound prosciutto or ham,
    chopped fine
1/4 pound mortadella, chopped fine
1/2 pound ground veal
2 mild Italian sausages, skinned
    and chopped
1 (10 ounce) package frozen
    chopped spinach, thawed
1 teaspoon minced garlic
2 tablespoons chopped fresh parsley

1/4 teaspoon grated lemon peel
1/4 teaspoon nutmeg
1/2 medium onion, chopped
3 eggs
1/4 teaspoon salt
1/4 teaspoon freshly ground black
    pepper
1/4 cup freshly grated Parmesan
    cheese
1/2 cup bread crumbs
Salt and pepper
1/3 cup olive oil
1/2 cup dry white wine
1/2 cup chicken broth

Place the veal flat on a large platter.

For the stuffing, soak the bread in the milk and then lightly squeeze some of the moisture out of it. In a large bowl, mix the prosciutto, mortadella, ground veal, and sausage. Add the chopped spinach, the soaked bread, garlic, parsley, lemon peel, nutmeg, and chopped onion. Beat the eggs with the salt and pepper, and add to the meat mixture along with the Parmesan cheese and bread crumbs. Lightly combine the meat mixture.

Stuff the veal breast tightly with the meat mixture until it is evenly thick and about 3 inches above the ribs. Sew the pocket together with a large needle and coarse cotton thread. Sprinkle the breast of veal on both sides with salt and pepper and place it in a large ovenproof pan with the olive oil, turning the veal once to coat it with the oil.

Brown the meat in a preheated 400° oven for about 15 minutes, turning it to brown both sides. Then add the wine and the broth and continue to roast the veal, pocket side up. Lower the oven temperature to 300° and roast the veal for about 1½ to 2 hours. Baste with pan juices every 30 minutes. The veal is done as soon as it is browned all over and very tender when pricked with a fork. Remove the veal from the oven and let it stand for 10 minutes before carving.

Transfer the meat to a cutting board and turn it with the ribs facing you. With a sharp knife, slice between the ribs and arrange them on a warm platter.

Remove some of the fat from the pan and add 2 tablespoons water. Cook the pan juices over medium heat, scraping up any cooking residue from the bottom of the pan with a wooden spoon, and continue cooking for few minutes. Then pour pan juices over the meat or serve the juices in a gravy bowl.

SERVES 10

~ *Patate con Funghi al Forno* ~
Baked Potatoes with Mushrooms

1½ cups dried porcini mushrooms or 1 pound fresh shiitake mushrooms, cleaned and cut in thin slices
6 tablespoons olive oil
3 medium onions, sliced thin
½ cup small strips of pancetta or bacon

3 pounds baking potatoes, peeled and cut in thin slices
Salt and freshly ground black pepper
1 cup freshly grated Parmesan cheese
2 cups milk

If using dried mushrooms, soak them in warm water for 20 minutes. Then rinse, drain, and squeeze them dry, and cut them into strips.

Sauté the mushrooms in a frying pan in 1 tablespoon of the olive oil over low heat for 5 minutes. In another frying pan, sauté the onions and pancetta or bacon over low heat in 3 tablespoons of the olive oil, until the onions are limp, for about 10 minutes.

Use the remaining 2 tablespoons of olive oil to coat a large baking dish and layer the potatoes, onion mixture, and mushrooms alternately. Sprinkle salt and pepper and Parmesan cheese over each mushroom layer. Pour the milk over the potatoes and bake in a preheated 350° oven for 50 minutes to 1 hour. The liquid should be absorbed and a light golden crust formed on top. Let the casserole rest for 5 minutes before serving.

SERVES 10

~ *Asparagi Saltati* ~
Sautéed Asparagus

3 pounds medium asparagus
1 large onion, thinly sliced
4 tablespoons (½ stick) sweet butter
3 tablespoons extra virgin olive oil
½ teaspoon salt

¼ teaspoon freshly ground black
  pepper
¼ teaspoon paprika
½ cup freshly grated Parmesan
  cheese

Cut the ends off each asparagus until the tender part is reached. Remove small leaves below the tip of the spear. Wash the asparagus in cold water and dry with paper towels. Cut each asparagus stalk at an angle into 1-inch pieces.

In a large frying pan, heat the butter and oil. When the butter starts to foam, add the onion and the cut asparagus. Cook over medium heat turning the asparagus with a wooden spoon several times. Sprinkle salt, pepper, and paprika over the asparagus when half cooked, about 7 to 10 minutes. Continue cooking and stirring until the asparagus is cooked but still al dente, for a total of about 15 to 20 minutes depending on the thickness of the asparagus.

Sprinkle the asparagus with the grated Parmesan cheese and continue cooking and turning it for another minute. Transfer the asparagus to a large heated serving dish. Serve at room temperature.

SERVES 10

~ *Torta di Zabaglione* ~
Zabaglione Cake

*18 ladyfingers, about 1½ 3-ounce
    packages*
6 egg yolks
1 cup sugar
1½ envelopes unflavored gelatin
½ cup Marsala wine

2 cups whipping cream
*1½ ounces semisweet chocolate,
    grated*
1 pint strawberries
2 tablespoons sugar

Split the ladyfingers in half. Line the bottom and sides of a 9-inch buttered springform pan with the split ladyfingers.

Beat the egg yolks with sugar until thick and lemon colored. Soften the gelatin in ½ cup cold water and dissolve over hot water. Add to egg mixture and then add the Marsala. Whip the cream until stiff and fold into egg mixture. Pour the custard into the prepared pan. Garnish with grated chocolate. Refrigerate. (This dessert can be made two or three days ahead. It will also keep nicely in the freezer for up to a month.)

Before serving, cut the strawberries in thick slices and mix them with the sugar. Place strawberry slices on top of the cake.

SERVES 10 to 12

Una Cena d'Estate alla Brace
A Summer Barbecue

Tagliatelle con Salsa di Melanzane
Tagliatelle with Eggplant Sauce

Grigliata Mista di Carne
Mixed Grilled Meats

Peperonata
Braised Peppers

Fagiolini e Patate alla Genovese
String Beans and Potatoes Genoa Style

Frutta d'Estate con Crema e Amaretto
Summer Fruit with Amaretto Liqueur Custard

Caffè Espresso
Espresso

SERVES 6

To me summer means casual entertaining—going on picnics and preparing numerous barbecue dinners for friends and family. In preparing the accompanying dishes for a summer barbecue, I usually take advantage of the many vegetables that are available. The tagliatelle with eggplant is a very flavorful, aromatic, and colorful dish.

The meats for the mixed grill are marinated in a variety of sauces, which provide unique flavors for them. The Peperonata (Braised Peppers) add color and contrasting flavors to the entrée. The recipe for the string beans and potatoes is an original of my husband's grandmother who lived in Genoa. The sautéed pancetta adds additional flavor to the string beans and potatoes.

Fresh fruit with custard is a cooling and refreshing ending to this summer barbecue.

Preparations

To avoid last minute preparations for your summer barbecue, you can prepare the eggplant sauce for the tagliatelle in the morning and reheat it before cooking the pasta just before dinner. The three sauces for the meats may be made early in the afternoon and poured over the meats so that they can marinate for several hours. The Peperonata can be made a day ahead and refrigerated. It may be served either at room temperature or warmed.

The string beans and potatoes should be served warm. Time permitting the beans may be cleaned and the potatoes peeled about one hour before cooking and placed in a dish with cold water. You can also sauté the pancetta and onion ahead and set them aside. When the beans and potatoes are cooked, the dish can be assembled and may sit for a few minutes so that the flavors can meld.

The Amaretto Liqueur Custard may be prepared one day ahead and refrigerated. However, it is wise not to slice the peaches or strawberries until serving time, since the peaches will discolor and the strawberries will lose some of their juiciness.

~ *Tagliatelle con Salsa di Melanzane* ~
Tagliatelle with Eggplant Sauce

¾ pound eggplant
Salt
4 tablespoons extra virgin olive oil
½ cup chopped pancetta or bacon
1 onion, chopped
1 celery stalk, chopped
2 cloves garlic, finely chopped
1 tablespoon capers, drained and
    chopped
5 green olives, pits removed,
    chopped
Pinch of red pepper flakes

¼ cup dry white wine
1 (28 ounce) can Italian tomatoes,
    tomatoes chopped fine and juice
    reserved
3 tablespoons chopped fresh parsley
4 tablespoons chopped fresh basil
¼ teaspoon salt
¼ teaspoon freshly ground black
    pepper
1 pound tagliatelle
½ cup freshly grated Parmesan
    cheese

Wash the eggplant and cut it into small cubes, without peeling it. Place the eggplant in a colander, sprinkle with salt, and let it sit for half an hour. (This procedure will remove the bitter juices from the eggplant.) Then rinse and dry the eggplant with paper towels.

Heat 2 tablespoons of the oil in a large frying pan over medium heat. Add the eggplant and cook it for a few minutes, turning it often. Do not let the eggplant brown. Remove the eggplant and drain it on paper towels. Heat the remaining 2 tablespoons oil in the same frying pan and add the pancetta, onion, celery, garlic, olives, and red pepper flakes. Sauté lightly for a few minutes. Add wine, chopped tomatoes and their liquid, cooked eggplant, parsley and basil. Season with salt and freshly ground black pepper and mix thoroughly.

Cook the tagliatelle in a large pot of boiling salted water until just tender but still firm to the bite. Simmer the sauce while the pasta is cooking. Drain the pasta, place it in a warm bowl or on a warm platter, and add the sauce and the grated cheese. Toss well and serve at once.

SERVES 6

~ Grigliata Mista di Carne ~
Mixed Grilled Meat

6 lamb chops
6 veal chops
6 half breasts of chicken, boneless
6 Italian sausages
Salt and freshly ground black pepper

LAMB CHOP MARINADE:

4 tablespoons olive oil
1 tablespoon chopped chives
½ teaspoon chopped fresh oregano
1 teaspoon chopped fresh parsley
1 clove garlic, chopped
3 tablespoons brandy

VEAL CHOP MARINADE:

4 tablespoons olive oil
2 cloves garlic, chopped
2 teaspoons chopped fresh rosemary
1 tablespoon dry white wine

CHICKEN BREAST MARINADE:

4 tablespoons olive oil
1 tablespoon chopped fresh herbs,
    (rosemary, sage, parsley, and
    marjoram)
2 cloves garlic, cut in thin slices

Place the lamb chops on a platter. Combine the marinade ingredients in a small bowl and pour the sauce over the lamb chops. Marinate for 3 hours.

Place the veal chops on a platter. Combine all of the veal marinade ingredients in a small bowl and pour the sauce over the veal chops. Marinate for 2 hours.

Place the chicken breasts on a platter. Combine the chicken marinade ingredients in a small bowl and pour over the chicken breasts. Marinate for 2 hours.

To cook the mixed grill, make sure the grill has been properly heated before adding the meats. Start cooking the chicken first since it takes longer to cook than the other meats, about 15 to 20 minutes or about 8 minutes per side, depending on the thickness of the meat. The Italian sausages, which do not need to be marinated, cook in 10 minutes. Before placing the sausages on the grill, prick their skin with a fork. This will prevent them from popping. Cook the sausage for about 10 minutes. If overcooked, they will get too dry. The lamb and veal chops should be added to the grill last since their cooking time is about 8 minutes, 4 minutes per side, depending on thickness of meat and desired doneness.

While the meats are cooking, brush them with some of their marinade. Season the meats with salt and pepper after they are cooked.

SERVES 6

~ *peronata* ~
...ed Peppers

...ut

1 large red onion, peeled and
    coarsely chopped

2 medium ripe tomatoes, peeled and
    chopped
¼ teaspoon red pepper flakes
½ teaspoon salt
¼ teaspoon freshly ground black
    pepper

Remove the stems and seeds from the peppers and julienne them.

Heat the oil in a large frying pan and add the garlic. Sauté the garlic until golden, then discard it. Add the chopped onion and sauté over medium heat for about 4 minutes. Add the peppers and sauté until the onions are lightly golden and the peppers have softened, about 10 minutes. Then add the chopped tomatoes, crushed pepper flakes, salt, and pepper and stir thoroughly. Cook for another 8 to 10 minutes on low heat, stirring occasionally, or until the peppers are soft. Add additional salt if needed. Transfer the Peperonata to a serving dish and serve either hot or cold.

SERVES 6

~ *Fagiolini e Patate alla Genovese* ~
String Beans and Potatoes Genoa Style

1½ pounds fresh young green beans
3 medium potatoes
3 tablespoons unsalted butter
4 tablespoons olive oil
1 medium onion, coarsely chopped
¼ pound lean pancetta or lean
    bacon, chopped

1 clove garlic, minced
2 tablespoons chopped fresh parsley
½ teaspoon salt
¼ teaspoon freshly ground black
    pepper

Snap both ends off the green beans, pulling away any strings, and soak them in cold water for 30 minutes. Peel and cut the potatoes into large cubes and rinse them under cold water.

Cook the beans and potatoes in a large saucepan in lightly salted water for 12 to 15 minutes. The beans and potatoes should be cooked but still firm.

Place the butter and oil in a large sauté pan and when the butter is melted, add the onion and pancetta. Sauté over medium heat until the onion is limp and the pancetta starts turning golden. Add the chopped garlic and parsley and the drained string beans and potatoes. Season with salt and pepper, mix thoroughly, and sauté very lightly for 2 to 3 minutes. Transfer the string beans and potatoes to a serving dish and serve warm with the grilled meats.

SERVES 6

~ *Frutta d'Estate con Crema e Amaretto* ~
Summer Fruit with Amaretto Liqueur Custard

2 cups half-and-half
½ cup whipping cream
5 egg yolks
¼ cup sugar
1 teaspoon vanilla extract

2 tablespoon Amaretto liqueur
3 large peaches, peeled, pitted, and thinly sliced
1½ cups fresh strawberries, sliced
6 mint leaves, for garnish

Combine the half-and-half and the heavy cream in a medium saucepan and cook over medium heat until bubbles form around the edge, about 3 minutes.

Beat the egg yolks and sugar in a large bowl until the mixture is thick and pale, about 2 minutes. Slowly beat in the cream. Return this mixture to the saucepan, add the vanilla extract, and continue cooking over low heat, stirring constantly, until the custard is thick enough to coat a wooden spoon, about 10 minutes. Do not allow it to boil.

Remove the custard from the heat, stir in the Amaretto liqueur, and whisk the custard for 2 to 3 minutes. Transfer it to a bowl, let it cool slightly, and then cover the bowl and refrigerate the custard until cold. (You can prepare the dessert to this point up to one day ahead.)

When ready to serve, spoon the custard into 6 individual shallow glass bowls. Arrange the sliced peaches and strawberries on top of each serving. Garnish with a mint leaf and serve.

SERVES 6

Una Serata in Autunno
An Evening in Autumn

Pappardelle con Salsa di Funghi
Pappardelle with Mushroom Sauce

Fette di Tacchino con tre Formaggi
Turkey Slices Folded with Three Cheeses

Zucchine Salate con Pancetta e Cipolla
Sautéed Zucchini with Pancetta and Onion

Pere Cotte al Forno
Baked Pears

Caffè
Coffee

SERVES 6

Autumn is the time of year when the leaves change color, the days start to get shorter, and the evenings are chilly. It is also the season when special ingredients, such as porcini mushrooms and pears, are readily available.

In Italy the main crop of porcini mushrooms, which grow wild, are picked from September to November, although some are also picked in the spring. Porcini mushrooms always remind me of autumn, and that is why I chose to feature them in this menu. Unfortunately we cannot get fresh porcini mushrooms in this country, thus I am using dried ones in the pasta dish. The combination of fresh mushrooms and dried porcini helps to create a flavorful sauce with an exquisite aroma for the pappardelle. Pappardelle, one of the traditional pasta shapes of Tuscany, are wide noodles, which are usually cut with a fluted pastry wheel.

For the main course three cheeses are combined with mild Italian sausage to stuff slices of turkey. They are sautéed and served with a light wine sauce. Sautéed zucchini is served as an accompaniment.

Since fruit is a typical ending to an Italian meal, I have chosen autumn pears for the finale. They are baked in red wine.

Preparations

In order to make your autumn entertaining easier, many items in this menu may be prepared in advance. The mushroom sauce for the pappardelle (wide noodles) may be made the day before and stored in the refrigerator. The evening of the dinner heat the sauce while the pasta is cooking.

To make your dinner preparations simpler, the turkey slices can be prepared in the morning, folded, and placed in the refrigerator. The turkey slices can be cooked just before your guests are to arrive. Then cover them and set them aside. Five minutes before dinner, warm the turkey.

The zucchini may also be prepared in advance. In the afternoon, clean and cut the zucchini and the onion. Cook the bacon as directed and cook the onion and zucchini on high heat for only 5 minutes of the cooking time. Remove the zucchini from the heat immediately to stop the cooking process. Then add the crumbled bacon and set aside. Ten minutes before dinner, finish cooking the zucchini and add the seasonings and cheese.

The pears may be baked the day before, covered, and refrigerated. If you plan to serve them at room temperature, remove them from the refrigerator 1 hour before serving.

~ *Pappardelle con Salsa di Funghi* ~
Pappardelle with Mushroom Sauce

2 ounces dried porcini mushrooms
1 cup warm water
1 pound small white mushrooms, thinly sliced
2 tablespoons butter
4 tablespoons olive oil
1 onion, finely chopped
2 cloves garlic, chopped
2 tablespoons chopped fresh parsley
2 tablespoons chopped fresh basil
½ teaspoon salt

¼ teaspoon freshly ground black pepper
½ cup dry white wine
4 large ripe fresh tomatoes, peeled and chopped or 2 cups canned Italian tomatoes with juice, tomatoes chopped
1 cup whipping cream
1 pound pappardelle (wide egg noodles)
½ cup freshly grated Parmesan cheese

Soak the dried porcini in one cup of warm water for 30 minutes. Strain and rinse the porcini and cut them into small pieces. Filter and save ½ cup of the porcini water for later use.

Melt the butter and olive oil in a medium saucepan over medium heat. Add the onion and sauté until limp. Add all of the mushrooms and the garlic and sauté for 5 minutes on high heat. Then add the parsley, basil, salt, pepper, wine, tomatoes, and the ½ cup of porcini water. Stir well to combine. Bring the sauce to a boil and simmer uncovered for 15 minutes. Add the cream and simmer for a few more minutes.

Just before adding the tomatoes, begin cooking the pasta until it is al dente. Drain the pasta, place it in a warm bowl or on a warm platter, and add the sauce and the grated cheese. Toss well and serve at once.

SERVES 6

~ *Fette di Tacchino con tre Formaggi* ~
Turkey Slices Folded with Three Cheeses

12 slices turkey breast
3 mild Italian sausages, skinned and crumbled
6 thin slices mozzarella cheese, cut in half
6 thin slices Fontina cheese, cut in half
6 thin slices provolone cheese, cut in half

12 large fresh sage leaves
Salt and freshly ground black pepper
4 tablespoons (½ stick) butter
½ cup dry white wine
1 cup chicken broth

Flatten the turkey slices with a mallet or rolling pin between two pieces of wax paper until thin. Spread a heaping tablespoon of sausage on half of each slice of turkey. Then top the sausage with one-half slice each of mozzarella, Fontina, and provolone cheese. Place a sage leaf on top of the cheese. Fold the other half of the turkey slice over the stuffing, close the "turkey package" with toothpicks to which a sage leaf has been attached, and season on both sides with salt and pepper.

Heat the butter in a large skillet over medium heat and when it starts to foam, add the stuffed turkey slices. Sauté on both sides until golden. Add the wine and let it evaporate over high heat. Then add the chicken broth. Cover the skillet and cook over low heat for a few minutes, until some of the melted cheese starts to peek out of the turkey.

Place the turkey slices on a warm platter. Cook the juices over high heat for a few minutes, scraping loose any residue that has stuck to the skillet. Pour these cooking juices into a small sauceboat. Serve each turkey slice with some of the sauce.

SERVES 6

~ *Zucchine Salate con Pancetta e Cipolla* ~
Sautéed Zucchini with Pancetta and Onion

5 medium firm zucchini
2 strips pancetta or lean bacon
2 tablespoons butter
1 large onion, thinly sliced

Salt and freshly ground black
    pepper
1/3 cup freshly grated Parmesan
    cheese

Scrub the zucchini under cold running water until the skin is smooth. Cut off and discard both ends of the zucchini. Cut it into 1-inch diagonal slices and set aside.

Place the pancetta or bacon in a large sauté pan (large enough to accommodate all the zucchini slices without piling them up more than 1½ inches) and cook over medium heat. When the bacon is crisp, remove it, and place on a paper towel to drain. Add the butter and onion to the bacon fat and cook over medium heat until the onion is limp. Add the sliced zucchini and season with salt and pepper. Cook, uncovered, on high for 5 to 10 minutes, stirring often. The zucchini are done when they turn a light brown at the edges and are tender but not mushy.

While the zucchini are still al dente, add the cooked bacon, which has been broken into small pieces. Sprinkle with the Parmesan cheese, mix thoroughly, and serve at once.

SERVES 6

~ *Pere Cotte al Forno* ~
Baked Pears

6 firm Anjou or Bosc pears
4 cups dry red wine
1 cup Marsala wine

1 cup sugar
Grated rind of 1 lemon

Wash the pears but do not peel them, and pack them close together in a large ovenproof dish. Combine the wines, ½ cup sugar, and the lemon rind and pour over the pears. Bake at 350° for 35 minutes, basting several times. Sprinkle remaining ½ cup of sugar over pears and bake for another 10 minutes. If there is too much liquid, remove it to a saucepan and reduce it by boiling. Then pour thickened juice over the pears. Serve warm or at room temperature.

SERVES 6

Invito di Minestre d'Inverno
Invitation to Winter Soups

Minestra di Patate e Verza
Potato and Cabbage Soup

Zuppa di Lenticchie
Lentil Soup

Zuppa d'Orzo con Verdure
Barley Soup with Vegetables

Insalata Ricca
Rich Salad

Formaggi e Frutta
Cheese and Fruit

Caffè Espresso
Espresso

SERVES 6 to 8

In the chill of winter, soups are delicious and filling, and they give a sense of warmth to the body. Italian soups can be very simple or elaborate, depending on the type of meal and the occasion.

Although there are many types of soups, I chose very simple but hearty ones for this party. All of them are easy to make. An ideal accompaniment to these soups is slices of French bread, either plain or toasted. The prosciutto and cheese salad is a very tasty, rich, and colorful interlude to this informal meal. An assortment of Italian cheeses served with fresh apples, pears, and grapes is the typical way Italians conclude this type of casual fare. If desired, serve some additional French bread with the cheeses. Also, coarse bread goes well with the tangy flavor of the pecorino, which is made from sheep's milk.

Preparations

All of the soups for this informal party can be prepared well ahead. They may even be frozen, thawed, and reheated, and be simmering when your guests arrive. If you choose not to freeze the soups, they can all be prepared several days ahead, refrigerated, and reheated at serving time. Either way there are several hints you should follow if making these soups ahead. It is wise not to add the Parmesan cheese to the Potato and Cabbage Soup until just before serving time, since the cheese tends to become stringy upon reheating. In making the Lentil Soup ahead, do not add the pasta since in reheating it will tend to get overdone. Add the pasta and cook it at the time you are going to serve the soup. Then add the butter and Parmesan cheese. The same holds true for the peas, butter, and Parmesan cheese in the Barley Soup recipe. Also add them several minutes before serving.

For a casual atmosphere, serve the soups buffet style, placing each tureen on a warming tray, if available. Stack the soup bowls beside the tureens and let the guests help themselves.

On the afternoon of your soup party you can prepare parts of the salad. The endive and lettuce can be cleaned, put in a salad bowl, and refrigerated. The prosciutto and cheese can be cut, wrapped separately in plastic wrap, and stored in the refrigerator. You can also make the dressing ahead. At serving time, combine the salad ingredients, add the dressing, and serve.

In order to keep the apples and pears from turning color, it is best to prepare the cheese and fruit platter just before the end of the meal.

~ Minestr[
Potato a

1 large Savoy cabbage
3 tablespoons olive oil
¼ cup chopped pancetta or bac[
1 medium onion, chopped
2 cloves garlic, finely chopped
¼ cup chopped fresh parsley
4 medium potatoes, peeled and
    in cubes
8 cups chicken broth
¼ teaspoon salt

12 ounces dri[
4 tablespo[
½ cup [
1 m[
2[

Cut the cabbage in quarters, remove the central rib, and cut the leaves into thin strips.

Heat the olive oil in a large saucepan over medium heat; add the pancetta and onion and sauté for a few minutes. Then add the garlic, parsley, and cabbage and continue cooking until the cabbage is limp, stirring occasionally. Add the potatoes and continue cooking and stirring until the cabbage and potatoes have absorbed all the liquid. Add the chicken broth, salt, pepper, and fennel seeds and gently stir to combine the ingredients. Bring to a slow boil and cook, covered, over low heat for 1 hour. When cooked, add the butter and Parmesan cheese and stir to combine.

To serve, place one slice of toasted bread in each deep soup plate and pour the soup over it. Sprinkle some Parmesan cheese on top and serve immediately.

SERVES 6 to 8

~ Zuppa di Lenticchie ~
Lentil Soup

...ed lentils
...ons olive oil
...hopped pancetta or bacon
...dium onion, chopped
...celery stalks, chopped
2 cloves garlic, chopped
8 cups chicken broth
4 ounces small macaroni pasta or

small shells
1 tablespoon unsalted butter
2 tablespoons freshly grated
  Parmesan cheese
Salt, to taste
Freshly ground black pepper, to
  taste

Wash the lentils in cold water.

Heat the olive oil in a stock pot or a Dutch oven over medium heat and sauté the pancetta, onion, celery, and garlic for several minutes. Add the lentils along with the chicken broth. Cover pot, bring to a slow boil, and cook over medium heat for 1 hour or until lentils are tender.

Remove 1/3 of the lentils, place them in the bowl of a food processor, and purée them. Return the purée to the soup. Bring to a boil; add the pasta, and cook over medium heat until the pasta is al dente, 12 to 15 minutes. Remove the soup from the heat; add the butter and Parmesan cheese and mix well to blend. Season with salt, if desired, sprinkle with pepper, and serve immediately.

SERVES 6 to 8

~ Zuppa d'Orzo con Verdure ~
Barley Soup with Vegetables

3 tablespoons olive oil
1 onion, finely chopped
1/4 cup finely chopped pancetta or
  bacon
1 bay leaf
3/4 pound Savoy cabbage, cut into
  small strips
1/2 pound fresh spinach, stems
  removed and cut into strips

10 cups chicken broth
2/3 cup pearl barley
1 pound frozen petite peas, thawed
  and rinsed
2 tablespoons unsalted butter
Salt, to taste
4 tablespoons freshly grated
  Parmesan cheese

Heat the olive oil in a stock pot or Dutch oven over medium heat and add the onion, pancetta, and bay leaf. Sauté until the onion is limp. Add the cabbage and spinach to the pot; toss gently and sauté for a few minutes. When the vegetables are limp, add the broth. Cover the stock pot and cook over medium heat for 15 minutes.

Add the barley and mix thoroughly. Season the soup with salt, if desired, and cook, covered, on low heat for 1 hour or until the barley is tender. Add the peas and continue cooking for 5 to 8 minutes or until the peas are done. Remove from heat, add the butter and Parmesan cheese, and mix well to blend. Place the soup in a preheated soup tureen and serve immediately.

SERVES 6 to 8

~ *Insalata Ricca* ~
Rich Salad

1 medium head Belgian endive,
   sliced
1 large head butter lettuce, torn into
   bite-size pieces
2 medium tomatoes, sliced
1 small red onion, thinly sliced
4 ounces prosciutto, cut into thin
   strips

4 ounces provolone cheese, cut into
   small cubes
¼ cup olive oil
Juice of ½ lemon
¼ teaspoon salt
¼ teaspoon fresh ground black
   pepper

Place the endive, lettuce, tomatoes, onion, prosciutto, and provolone in a large salad bowl. Whisk together the olive oil, lemon juice, salt, and pepper in a small bowl. Pour dressing over salad and mix thoroughly.

SERVES 6 to 8

Formaggie Frutta
Cheese and Fruit

¼ to ⅓ pound wedges of fontina,
Gorgonzola, Parmesan, and
pecorino cheeses
3 apples

3 pears
2 large bunches grapes, cut into
individual servings
Red lettuce leaves, for garnish

Arrange the cheeses and fruits on a large serving platter. Garnish with the lettuce leaves. Just before serving, slice the apples and pears. Serve with French bread, if desired.

SERVES 6 TO 8

Menus for
Family and Friends

Un Pranzo di Pasta per l'Amiche
A Pasta Dinner for Pals

Picnic nella Foresta
A Picnic in the Forest

Un Invito per le Partite Sportive
Tailgate Party

Un Pranzo sotta la Pergola
Luncheon under the Arbor

Brunch Stile Italiano
Italian-Style Brunch

Polenta con Gusto
Polenta with Taste

Una Festa di Caccia
A Hunter's Feast

Un Pranzo per la Promessa Sposa
A Bridal Luncheon

Un Pranzo per le Laureate
A Luncheon for the Graduates

Una Cena di Famiglia
A Family Dinner

Festa delle Mamma
Mother's Day Feast

L'Festa del Papa
Father's Day Feast

Un Pranzo di Pasta per l'Amiche
A Pasta Dinner for Pals

Crostini con Prosciutto e Fontina
Breadsticks with Prosciutto and Fontina Cheese

Linguine al Salmone
Linguine with Salmon Sauce

Paglia e Fieno con Ragù
Yellow and Green Fettuccine with Meat Sauce

Penne con Peperoni e Salsicce
Penne with Peppers and Sausages

Insalata Mista
Mixed Salad

Dolce Torinese
Chocolate Loaf with Almonds

Caffè
Coffee

SERVES 12

This is a meal for pasta aficionados. It features seafood and meat sauces. Although salmon is not a fish of Italian origin, modern transportation has made it readily available to Italians. The Yellow and Green Fettuccine with Meat Sauce, which combines three different meats, is an eye-catching dish with the contrasting colors of the fettuccine, the green peas, and the tomato-based sauce. The Penne with Peppers and Sausages adds a spicy dimension to the dinner.

Preparations

This dinner is a host's dream because all of the major preparations can be done ahead. If you so desire, the two meat sauces can be prepared 3 or 4 days in advance, stored in the refrigerator, and reheated on the evening of the party. The salmon sauce, however, should be prepared in the late afternoon of your party since you will be using fresh salmon. After the sauce is finished it can be covered, set aside, and reheated before serving.

If your schedule permits, you may want to prepare the various salad greens in the morning and store them in plastic bags in the refrigerator. Before sitting down to dinner you can assemble the salad, add the hearts of palm, and make the dressing. You may also want to chop the avocado, but if doing so, sprinkle it with a little lemon juice to keep it from discoloring.

The appetizer can also be made several hours ahead. Simply wrap thin slices of prosciutto around bread sticks and cut cubes of cheese to go with them. Arrange them on a platter, cover with plastic wrap, and refrigerate. When your guests arrive you are ready to serve these tidbits with drinks.

Since the Chocolate Loaf with Almonds should be refrigerated for 4 hours before serving, it can actually be made a day ahead. However, the flavors will be best if it is not made more than 24 to 36 hours ahead of the party.

The evening of the party warm the sauces and keep them on simmering heat while you cook the pastas. Cook the penne first since it takes the longest. To make it easier to combine each pasta with its sauce, it a good idea to stagger the cooking of the pastas. Each cooked pasta may also be placed in a dish and tossed with the butter called for in the recipe, then covered with aluminum foil and placed in a warm (150° to 175°) oven. The pasta will keep for about 15 minutes without drying out or sticking together. Remember to cook your pasta al dente (firm to the teeth).

The three pasta dishes will each serve 12. However, if you plan to use just one of the recipes, it will be sufficient for 4 to 6, depending on what else you are serving. You might want to place a bowl of additional grated Parmesan cheese on the table for those wanting to sprinkle extra on top of the pastas.

~ *Crostini con Prosciutto e Fontina* ~
Breadsticks with Prosciutto and Fontina Cheese

24 breadsticks, or 12 Italian bread-
sticks, cut in half
24 thin slices prosciutto

¾ pound fontina cheese, cut into
1-inch cubes

Wrap the prosciutto around each breadstick leaving an area at one end unwrapped so that it can easily be held. Arrange the wrapped breadsticks on a platter with the cubes of cheese in the middle.

SERVES 12

~ *Linguine al Salmone* ~
Linguine with Salmon Sauce

6 tablespoons (¾ stick) unsalted
butter
1 clove garlic, peeled and cut in half
½ cup chopped red onion
½ cup small cubes of prosciutto
¾ pound fresh salmon filet, cut into
1-inch cubes
3 teaspoons chopped fresh parsley
2 tablespoons chopped fresh basil

2 cups canned Italian tomatoes
with juice, tomatoes chopped
¼ teaspoon salt
½ teaspoon freshly ground black
pepper
½ tablespoon extra virgin olive oil
½ cup whipping cream
1 pound linguine

Melt 4 tablespoons butter in a large saucepan over medium heat and add the garlic, sautéing it until brown. Then discard the garlic. Add the onions, prosciutto, and salmon, separating the salmon pieces with a fork as they cook. Continue cooking for 3 minutes. Then add the parsley, basil, tomatoes, salt, pepper, and olive oil and stir gently but thoroughly. Simmer the sauce uncovered for 10 minutes. Add the cream and simmer for another 5 minutes.

While the salmon sauce is simmering, cook the pasta until it is al dente. Drain the linguine and place it on a large heated platter. Add the sauce and the remaining 2 tablespoons butter. Toss and serve at once.

SERVES 12 for the pasta dinner or 4 to 6 entrées

~ *Paglia e Fieno con Ragù* ~
Yellow and Green Fettuccine with Meat Sauce

3 tablespoons butter
2 tablespoons extra virgin olive oil
1 stalk celery, finely chopped
1 medium onion, finely chopped
1 medium carrot, finely chopped
2 cloves garlic, chopped
3 tablespoon chopped fresh parsley
5 ounces ground veal
5 ounces lean ground beef (chuck)
5 ounces mild Italian sausages,
    casings removed, crumbled
1/3 cup chopped lean pancetta or
    bacon
1/4 teaspoon salt

1/2 teaspoon freshly ground black
    pepper
1 tablespoon dry Italian seasoning
Pinch red pepper flakes
1/2 cup dry white wine
1 (28 ounce) can Italian tomatoes
    with juice, tomatoes chopped
1 cup beef broth
1 cup peas, fresh or frozen
9 ounces spinach fettuccine
9 ounces egg fettuccine
2/3 cup freshly grated Parmesan
    cheese

Melt 1½ tablespoons of the butter with the olive oil in a Dutch oven or a large saucepan over medium heat. Add the celery, onion, carrot, garlic, and parsley and sauté lightly until the vegetables are soft, 3 to 5 minutes. Then add the veal, beef, sausage, and pancetta and continue sautéing until the meat is no longer pink.

Add the salt, pepper, Italian seasoning, red pepper flakes, and wine, stirring to combine. Continue cooking over medium-low heat until most of the liquids have evaporated, about 10 minutes. Then add the tomatoes and their juice and the beef broth; bring to a boil and simmer uncovered for 30 minutes, stirring the sauce occasionally. If any fat has accumulated on top of the sauce, remove it with a large spoon. (Sometimes Italian sausages have more fat than wanted.) Add the peas, cover, and continue cooking for 10 minutes.

Just before adding the peas, begin cooking the pasta until it is al dente. Drain the fettuccine, place it in a warm bowl, and add the remaining 1½ tablespoons of butter. Add the sauce and the grated cheese. Toss well and serve at once.

SERVES 12 for the pasta dinner or 4 to 6 entrées

~ *Penne con Peperoni e Salsicce* ~
Penne with Peppers and Sausages

*1 large clove garlic, peeled and cut
in half*
3 tablespoons olive oil
½ medium onion, chopped
*1 large red bell pepper, cut in small
cubes*
*1 large yellow bell pepper, cut in
small cubes*
*1 (28 ounce) can Italian peeled toma-
toes with juice, coarsely chopped*

and mixed with 1 cup water
½ teaspoon salt
½ teaspoon freshly ground pepper
Pinch red pepper flakes
*4 mild Italian sausages, casings
removed, crumbled*
2 tablespoons unsalted butter
*⅔ cup freshly grated Parmesan
cheese*
1 pound ridged penne pasta

Sauté the garlic in the olive oil in a large saucepan over medium heat until browned. Discard the garlic. Add the onions and peppers to the oil in the pan and cook about 7 minutes or until the onion is wilted. Add the tomatoes, salt, pepper, and red pepper flakes and cook for about 10 minutes over medium heat.

Place the sausage meat in another skillet with ¼ cup water. Cook the sausage over medium heat until it is lightly browned and the water has evaporated. Add the sausage meat along with 3 tablespoons of its fat to the sauce mixture. Cook over medium heat for 10 minutes.

While the sauce is cooking, begin boiling the pasta until al dente. Drain the penne well and transfer it to a warm platter. Add the butter, sauce, and Parmesan cheese. Toss thoroughly and serve at once.

SERVES 12 for the pasta dinner or 4 to 6 entrées

~ *Insalata Mista* ~
Mixed Salad

1 medium head romaine lettuce, cut julienne
1 medium head radicchio, cut julienne
2 large Belgian endive, cut into rounds
2 large bunches arugula, cut coarsely
1 fennel bulb, cut in small pieces
1 small red onion, chopped
1 (14 ounce) can hearts of palm, cut into rounds
1 large avocado, peeled, pitted, and cut into cubes
8 tablespoons extra virgin olive oil
2 tablespoons fresh lemon juice
2 tablespoons red wine vinegar
4 tablespoons freshly grated Parmesan cheese
Salt and freshly ground pepper

Combine the romaine, radicchio, endive, arugula, fennel, and onion in a large salad bowl. Just before serving add the hearts of palm and avocado.

To make the dressing, whisk together the olive oil, lemon, and vinegar in a small bowl. Season with salt and pepper to taste and add the Parmesan cheese. Pour the dressing over the salad and toss.

SERVES 12

~ *Dolce Torinese* ~
Chocolate Loaf with Almonds

½ *pound semisweet chocolate, in*
    small pieces
½ *cup rum*
½ *pound (2 sticks) unsalted butter,*
    softened
2 *tablespoons superfine sugar*
2 *eggs, separated*

1½ *cups grated blanched almonds*
    (about 5 ounces)
12 *butter, petite beurre, or social*
    tea biscuits, cut into 1 inch by
    ½ *inch pieces*
1 *cup whipping cream, whipped*

Lightly grease a 1½ quart loaf pan with cooking spray and invert the pan over paper towels to drain off the excess.

Melt chocolate in the top of a double boiler over hot, not boiling, water. When melted, stir in the rum and cool to room temperature. Cream the butter until fluffy and beat in sugar. Add the egg yolks, one at a time. Stir in the grated almonds and the cooled chocolate.

Beat the egg whites until stiff and fold them into the chocolate mixture. Gently fold in the biscuit pieces. Spoon the chocolate mixture into the pan and smooth the top. Cover with plastic wrap. Refrigerate for at least four hours.

To serve, unmold the chocolate loaf and slice it thin. Serve with a dollop of whipped cream.

SERVES 12

Picnic nella Foresta
A Picnic in the Forest

Tortino di Maccheroncini
Macaroni Pie

Panini Ripieni con Prosciutto
Rolls Stuffed with Prosciutto

Frittata di Spinaci
Spinach Frittata

Frutta di Stagione
Fruit in Season

Biscotti con Cioccolata e Noci
Cookies with Chocolate and Nuts

SERVES 6 to 8

The day after Easter, a traditional holiday in Italy, is usually spent in the forest. It marks the beginning of warm weather and outdoor recreation. Summer in Italy tends to be very hot, thus whole families like to get away from the heat to the coolness of a nearby forest. They spend the entire day there enjoying various recreational activities, such as hiking, playing ball, and gathering wildflowers. A delicious picnic lunch accompanies this outing. The picnic basket often contains pies and frittatas that can be prepared ahead, as well as some type of sandwiches. Fruit, a sweet, and sodas, beer, or bottles of white and red wine complete a relaxing repast.

In this country, too, we can take a trip to the country and find a stretch of cooling woods for a picnic.

Preparations

To enjoy a relaxing picnic in the forest, you can prepare much of the food ahead of the outing. Since both the Macaroni Pie and the

Spinach Frittata are delicious served cold, they can both be prepared the day before the excursion and refrigerated. However, if you are not going on a picnic, the Macaroni Pie or the Spinach Frittata may also be served warm for a luncheon or light supper. If you are leaving early in the day, the rolls may also be prepared the day before. Otherwise, they may also be prepared just before serving.

The cookies, which are flavored with Amaretto and rich in chocolate and nuts, can be baked a day or so ahead and kept in an airtight container. It might be wise to hide them from the rest of the family so that they do not disappear before the picnic. Prepare the fruit of your choice—apples, grapes, berries, or plums—just before you are ready to leave so that they will be fresh and not soggy. Buon Divertimento! (Have a good time!)

~ *Tortino di Maccheroncini* ~
Macaroni Pie

1 cup chopped onion
6 tablespoons olive oil
1 cup chopped peeled tomatoes with
    their juice
½ teaspoon salt
½ teaspoon freshly ground black
    pepper

½ cup chopped fresh basil
1 pound small macaroni
8 large eggs
4 ounces ham, cut in small cubes
4 ounces salami, cut in small cubes
¾ cup freshly grated Parmesan
    cheese

Sauté the onion in a small skillet with 3 tablespoons olive oil over medium heat until the onion is lightly colored. Add the tomatoes, ¼ teaspoon of the salt, ¼ teaspoon of the pepper, and the chopped basil and cook slowly on low heat for 10 minutes.

Boil the macaroni until al dente. Drain and mix the pasta with the tomatoes and set aside. Beat the eggs in a large bowl and combine them with the cubed ham and salami, the remaining ¼ teaspoon of salt, the remaining ¼ teaspoon of pepper, and ½ cup of the Parmesan cheese. Add the pasta and tomato mixture and mix.

Heat the remaining 3 tablespoons olive oil in a deep, heavy ovenproof 12-inch skillet. When hot, add the pasta mixture and smooth out the top with a spatula. Cook, covered, over low heat for 30 to 35 minutes. The eggs should be set and the top still runny. Sprinkle the remaining ¼ cup cheese over the top and place the skillet in an oven with the broiler preheated. Broil for 5 to 7 minutes, until the macaroni pie is golden in color and firm.

Slide the pie onto a large round platter and set it aside to cool. The macaroni pie may be served either hot or cold.

SERVES 6 TO 8

~ *Panini Ripieni con Prosciutto* ~
Rolls Stuffed with Prosciutto

1 (14 ounce) can small artichokes,
    whole hearts
2 tablespoons fresh chopped parsley
1 clove garlic, finely chopped
3 tablespoons extra virgin olive oil
¼ teaspoon salt

¼ teaspoon freshly ground black
    pepper
4 sourdough or sweet rolls
1 pound prosciutto, thinly sliced
6 ounces fontina or provolone
    cheese, thinly sliced

Prepare the artichokes one day ahead so that they can marinate in the oil. Drain the artichokes, cut them into thin slices, and place them in a small bowl. Add the chopped parsley, garlic, olive oil, salt, and pepper. Mix thoroughly, cover, and refrigerate.

The next day, split the rolls and remove some of the center of the bread from each half. Brush the inside of each half with some of the olive oil from the artichokes. Layer the prosciutto, the cheese, and the sliced artichokes on the bottom half of each roll. Cover with the top half of the roll and press down lightly. Cut each sandwich roll in half and wrap in plastic wrap, then in foil wrap, and refrigerate. These rolls may also be prepared just before serving.

SERVES 6 to 8

~ Frittata di Spinaci ~
Spinach Frittata

¾ pound fresh spinach
3 tablespoons olive oil
2 cloves garlic, chopped
2 slices pancetta or bacon, chopped
    fine
8 large eggs

¼ teaspoon salt
¼ teaspoon freshly ground black
    pepper
⅛ teaspoon nutmeg
¾ cup freshly grated Parmesan
    cheese

Wash and spin dry the spinach; remove stems and chop the leaves coarsely.

Heat the olive oil in a large ovenproof skillet over medium heat. Add the garlic and pancetta or bacon and sauté for a few minutes. Then add the spinach and cook, stirring often, until the spinach is wilted, about 2 to 3 minutes.

Beat the eggs in a medium bowl until frothy and add the salt, pepper, and nutmeg. Then stir in the cheese and mix to combine the ingredients.

Add the egg mixture to the spinach in the pan and mix lightly. Reduce the heat to low, cover the pan, and cook for 10 minutes until the eggs have set but the top is still runny. Place the skillet in an oven with the broiler preheated and broil for a couple of minutes, or until the frittata is golden. Slide the frittata onto a round serving platter. Cut into wedges and serve either hot or cold.

SERVES 6 to 8

~ *Biscotti con Cioccolata e Noci* ~
Cookies with Chocolate and Nuts

1 cup light brown sugar, firmly
    packed
1 cup granulated sugar
2 cups (4 sticks) butter
½ cup Amaretto liqueur
½ teaspoon salt
1 tablespoon vanilla

4 eggs
4½ cups flour
1¼ tablespoons baking soda
4 cups chocolate chips
1 cup pecans, lightly toasted
1 cup walnuts, lightly toasted

Cream the sugars and butter with an electric mixer. Add the Amaretto liqueur, salt, and vanilla. Then add the eggs, one at a time, mixing well after each addition. Combine the flour and baking soda and add to the egg mixture. Fold in the chocolate chips and then the nuts.

Place the dough by tablespoonfuls on an ungreased baking sheet. Bake in a preheated 375° oven for 8 to 10 minutes or until the cookies are lightly browned. Cool the cookies on racks before storing them in an airtight container.

5 to 6 dozen large cookies

Un Invito per le Partite Sportive
An Invitation to a Tailgate Party

Frittata di Riso
Rice Frittata

Polpettone
Meat Loaf

Fagioli con Luganega
Beans with Sausages

Insalata di Cetrioli
Cucumber Salad

Torta d'Arancia
Orange Cake

SERVES 6 to 8

Although the only foods usually available at sporting events in Italy are hot roasted chestnuts, sporting events are as popular in Italy as they are in this country. Soccer attracts the attention in Italy, and here it is football—high school, college, or professional. All of them create excitement and a party atmosphere. In this country tailgate parties before a football game have become the norm. They are an ideal and informal way for friends to get together and enjoy the anticipated excitement of their team winning the game.

Even though tailgate parties are not the custom in Italy, I have selected an Italian menu for this occasion. The Rice Frittata may be served as an appetizer, either cut in wedges or in smaller squares to share with other tailgaters around you. Meat Loaf is as popular here as it is in Italy. For the tailgate party it may be served sliced, used to make a sandwich, or slices of it may be topped with the hot Beans with Sausage. If the day is a cold one, the hot Beans with Sausage will be a welcome addition to the meal.

Luganega, a mild sausage, is the basis of many Italian dishes including stews, risottos, and various bean dishes. In Italy, it is sold by length rather than by weight. In the Fagioli con Luganega I have used the more readily available mild Italian sausages.

The Cucumber Salad offers a light contrast to the more substantial Meat Loaf and beans. Soft drinks, beer, or wine may accompany this meal for hearty appetites.

Slices of the moist Orange Cake with a glass of white wine will complete this tailgate party.

Preparations

If you and your family or friends are attending a fall football game, you will probably be busy on the morning of the game assembling warm clothes, maybe some umbrellas, and a blanket or two. Then there is the thermos of hot coffee to prepare.

To avoid the last minute rush of food preparation for the tailgate party, you may prepare all of the dishes for this menu a day or two ahead. The Rice Fritatta should be the last item on the menu to be prepared before the game, either on the afternoon of the day before the event or that morning. The Meat Loaf and the Beans with Sausage can be cooked a day or two in advance. You will want to refrigerate all of these dishes, and maybe reheat the Meat Loaf in a 200° oven for about 20 minutes before you leave for the game. Or you can reheat it in the microwave for about 5 minutes.

To counteract the autumn chill at the tailgate party, you will want to serve the Beans with Sausage hot. Heat them to boiling just before leaving, put them in a heated serving dish and wrap it in newspapers and a blanket. The beans will stay warm for quite a while. If you cook them in a crock pot and have a converter for the cigarette lighter in the car, you can keep them warm all the way to the game.

Prepare the Cucumber Salad ingredients a day ahead, place them in a salad bowl, and store in the refrigerator. Also you can make the dressing a day ahead and pour it over the salad just before leaving for the game.

The Orange Cake can be prepared at your leisure two days in advance, since it needs that time to absorb the topping, which makes the cake moist. Whip the cream just before you leave and take it in a cooler.

~ *Frittata di Riso* ~
Rice Frittata

2 cups chicken broth
1 cup Italian Arborio rice
5 tablespoons unsalted butter
2 bunches scallions, white parts
    only, chopped
2 leeks, white parts only, chopped
6 large eggs

¼ teaspoon nutmeg
½ teaspoon salt
½ teaspoon freshly ground black
    pepper
½ cup freshly grated Parmesan
    cheese

Bring the chicken broth to a boil in a medium saucepan and add the rice. Stir, cover the pan, and cook on low heat for 15 minutes, or until the rice is al dente. Set aside to cool.

Melt 4 tablespoons butter in a skillet over medium heat, and when it starts to foam add the chopped scallions and leeks. Sauté, stirring often, for about 10 minutes. Remove the skillet from the heat, add the cooked rice, and mix.

Beat the eggs in a large bowl with the nutmeg and pepper until foamy and then add the Parmesan cheese. Add the rice to the egg mixture and combine thoroughly.

Heat the remaining tablespoon of butter in a large skillet. When the butter is foaming, pour in the egg mixture and smooth out the top. Cook, covered, over low heat for 10 minutes, or until the eggs begin to thicken. Remove the pan and place it, uncovered, in a preheated 300° broiler. Broil for about 3 minutes or until the top is golden and the eggs are completely set. When the fritatta is cooked, slide it onto a serving platter. Cut it into wedges like a pie and serve either hot or cold. The frittata may also be cut in small squares and served as an hors d'oeuvre.

SERVES 6 to 8

~ *Polpettone* ~
Meat Loaf

2 celery stalks, chopped
1 carrot, chopped
1 medium onion, chopped
2 cloves garlic, chopped
2 tablespoons chopped fresh parsley
4 tablespoons unsalted butter
2 tablespoons olive oil
1 pound ground beef (chuck)
½ pound ground veal
3 mild Italian sausages (½ pound),
    casings removed

3 slices white bread, crusts re-
    moved, soaked in ½ cup of milk
2 eggs, beaten
½ teaspoon salt
½ teaspoon freshly ground black
    pepper
¼ teaspoon nutmeg
1 teaspoon grated lemon rind
½ cup Parmesan cheese
1 (8 ounce) can tomato sauce
1 cup bread crumbs

Heat 3 tablespoons butter and the oil in a large skillet over medium heat. Add the celery, carrot, onion, garlic, and parsley and sauté until all the vegetables are soft. Remove from heat and let cool.

Combine the ground beef, veal, sausage meat, and the sautéed vegetables in a large bowl. Add the soaked bread and mix with a wooden spoon.

Beat the eggs with the salt, pepper, and nutmeg in another bowl. Add the lemon rind and Parmesan cheese and mix thoroughly. Then add the egg mixture to the meat. Stir in ½ can tomato sauce and add the bread crumbs. Mix thoroughly with a wooden spoon or with your hands and form into a large loaf.

Butter a rectangular ovenproof pan with the remaining 1 table-spoon butter. Place the meat loaf in the pan, smooth out the top, and pour the remaining ½ can tomato sauce on top. Bake in a preheated 350° oven for 1 hour. Remove the meat loaf from the pan and place it on a serving platter. Let it cool. Cut the meat loaf into slices when ready to serve. The meat loaf may also be served warm.

SERVES 6 to 8

~ *Fagioli con Luganega* ~
Beans with Sausage

1 pound dry white beans
5 tablespoons olive oil
¾ pound lean pork loin, cut in
    small pieces
4 ounces pancetta or bacon, finely
    chopped
1 onion, finely chopped
2 cloves garlic, finely chopped
1 tablespoon chopped fresh
    rosemary

1 tablespoon chopped fresh sage
1 can (14½ ounces) peeled Italian
    tomatoes, chopped, reserve juice
2 cups chicken broth
¼ teaspoon salt
¼ teaspoon freshly ground black
    pepper
8 Italian sausages, mild or hot
3 large sage leaves

Soak the beans overnight. Drain and cook them in plenty of salted water until cooked, but still al dente. Do not overcook. In a large casserole with 4 tablespoons olive oil, over medium heat, sauté the pork pieces and the chopped pancetta for about 4 minutes. Add chopped onion, garlic, rosemary, and sage, mix, and continue cooking until the onion is limp. Add the chopped tomatoes, broth, and salt and pepper. Mix all together, bring to a boil, cover the casserole, and cook over low heat for 30 minutes. In another skillet with 1 tablespoon olive oil, sauté the sausages (which you have pricked with a fork) for 10 minutes, turning them often so that they can brown on all sides. Add the sausages and the drained, cooked white beans to the casserole with the sage leaves. Mix gently, cover, and cook slowly for another 20 minutes. Arrange the sausages and beans with the sauce on a large preheated platter and serve hot.

SERVES 8

~ *Insalata di Cetrioli* ~
Cucumber Salad

1 *medium red onion, sliced thin*
2 *large cucumbers, sliced thin*
4 *firm, slightly under-ripened*
    Roma tomatoes, cut into ½ inch
    thick wedges, seeds removed

10 *fresh basil leaves, broken into*
    pieces
$^1/_3$ *cup extra virgin olive oil*
3 *tablespoons red wine vinegar*
Salt and freshly ground pepper

Put the sliced onions in a bowl and cover with cold water. Let stand for 7 minutes, then drain. Repeat this process 3 more times. This removes some of the strong onion taste. Drain the onions and pat dry with paper towels.

Combine the salad ingredients in a bowl. Make the dressing by whisking together the oil and vinegar and add salt and pepper to taste. Pour the dressing over the salad and serve.

SERVES 6 to 8

~ *Torta d'Arancia* ~
Orange Cake

6 egg yolks, room temperature
1 cup sugar
3 tablespoons cold water
1 cup flour

1 teaspoon baking powder
6 egg whites
Dash salt

Beat the egg yolks, sugar, and water together until thick and lemon colored. Combine the flour and baking powder and fold into the egg yolks. Beat the 6 egg whites with a dash of salt until they hold stiff peaks. Fold the egg whites into the batter and gently pour it into an ungreased, parchment-lined 9½-inch springform pan. Bake in a preheated 350° oven for 50 minutes or until a wire cake tester inserted in the center comes out clean. Let the cake cool in the oven with the door open. When cold, remove the rim of the pan and turn the cake upside down on a large playe, remove the paper, and trim any top crust. Prick the cake all over with the prongs of a fork.

TOPPING:

8 tablespoons superfine sugar
1 cup frozen concentrated orange
   juice, thawed
Juice of 1 lemon

Grated rind of 1 lemon
Grated rind of 1 orange
1 cup whipping cream

Combine the orange juice, lemon juice, and lemon and orange rinds, and either stir vigorously with a spoon or whisk to incorporate and dissolve the sugar. Spoon this topping slowly onto the cake by spoonfuls over a period of time until all the topping is absorbed. This will take about 20 minutes.

To serve, whip the cream and spread it in a thin layer on top of the cake.

SERVES 8 to 10

Un Pranzo sotto la Pergola
Luncheon under the Arbor

Insalata di Pasta
Pasta Salad

Frittate a Strati
Layers of Frittate

Insalata di Tonno e Fagioli
Tuna and Bean Salad

Torta di Limone con Noci
Lemon Cake with Walnuts

Caffè
Coffee

SERVES 8

Since Italy has numerous vineyards, as well as home grape arbors, many summer luncheons are served outdoors under the cooling leaves of a grape arbor. It gives one the feeling of being in a vineyard, yet protected from the sun's hot rays. In honor of the wine-making of Italy and California, where I now live, I have planned a luncheon to be served under the arbor.

I suggest you start the luncheon with a cool glass of white wine. The menu I have selected includes two cold salads and a light fritatta, all in keeping with the prospect of a warm day. The Pasta Salad includes a variety of colorful vegetables to reflect the gay mood of summer. A slightly tart Lemon Walnut Cake ends this leisurely lunch. Another glass of wine would be a nice complement to the cake.

Preparations

You will find that this is a very easy menu to prepare. Cook the pasta the day before, drain, and rinse it. Then toss the pasta with 1 tablespoon of olive oil and store it in the refrigerator. The vegetables, ham, and cheese can be cut and prepared the day before. You may also want to make the dressing in advance since this will give the flavors a chance to blend. On the morning of the luncheon, assemble the salad and toss it with the dressing. The Tuna and Bean Salad can be completely assembled on the day before the luncheon.

The Layers of Fritatte should be prepared just before the guests arrive and served at room temperature. You can let the assembled frittate rest while you and your guests are enjoying a glass of wine.

The Lemon Walnut Cake, which keeps very well, may be baked one or two days before the luncheon.

~ Insalata di Pasta ~
Pasta Salad

1 pound short elbow macaroni or fusilli

1 (6 ounce) jar mixed vegetables in vinegar, drained and rinsed

5 ounces boiled ham, cut in strips

5 ounces fontina cheese, cut in cubes

3 tablespoons pearl onions in vinegar, cut in half

1 medium red bell pepper, roasted, peeled, and sliced in ¼-inch strips (For roasting instructions see page 150), or 1 (6 ounce) jar sweet peppers in oil, sliced

1 (4 ounce) can button mushrooms, drained and rinsed

1 (3 ounce) jar maraschino cherries, sliced

¾ cup green seedless grapes

3 tablespoons capers

1 celery heart (4 stalks), sliced

1 large tomato, cut in thin strips, seeds removed

Freshly ground black pepper, optional

Prepare the dressing first (see recipe below). Then boil the pasta in salted water until al dente, drain it, and rinse under cold water. Then drain again thoroughly.

Place the cooked pasta in a large bowl, add the mixed vegetables, ham, fontina cheese, onions, red pepper, mushrooms, cherries, grapes, capers, celery, and tomato. Then add the dressing and mix thoroughly. If desired, sprinkle more freshly ground black pepper over the salad just before serving.

DRESSING:

4 tablespoons chopped fresh parsley

3 tablespoons chopped fresh basil

2 tablespoons watercress leaves

1 clove garlic, chopped

6 tablespoons extra virgin olive oil

Juice of one large lemon

½ teaspoon salt

½ teaspoon freshly ground black pepper

Place the parsley, basil, watercress leaves, and garlic in a small bowl. Add the olive oil, lemon juice, salt, and pepper and mix well. Cover and set aside to meld flavors while preparing the salad.

SERVES 8

~ Frittate a Strati ~
Layers of Frittate

1 eggplant (about ¾ pound)
12 eggs
½ teaspoon salt
½ teaspoon freshly ground black
   pepper
7 tablespoons freshly grated Parmesan cheese
4 tablespoons milk
5 tablespoons olive oil

2 mild Italian sausages, casings
   removed, meat crumbled
1 round (12 ounces) mozzarella
   cheese, cut in round slices
3 large tomatoes, cut in round
   slices, seeds removed
Freshly ground black pepper
10 basil leaves for decoration

Peel the eggplant, cut it in small cubes, and place in a colander. Sprinkle salt over the eggplant and let it sit for 10 minutes. This will remove the bitterness of the eggplant. Rinse the eggplant under running water and pat dry with a paper towel.

Beat the eggs in a large bowl with the salt, pepper, and Parmesan cheese. Add the milk and set aside for 10 minutes.

Heat 2 tablespoons of the oil in a large skillet, add the crumbled sausages and the eggplant cubes, and cook over medium heat, mixing often until the eggplant is soft and the sausage meat is slightly cooked.

Divide the beaten eggs into 3 equal parts in 3 bowls; add 1/3 of the cooked sausage and eggplant mixture to each bowl and mix well.

Since you will be cooking 3 omelets of the same size, begin by putting 1 tablespoon of the olive oil in a medium ovenproof skillet and heating the oil. When the oil is hot, add one of the egg mixtures to the skillet, cover, reduce the heat to low, and cook for 5 minutes or until the eggs have set and just the top is runny. Place the uncovered skillet in the oven under a preheated broiler for a few minutes or until the fritatta is golden. Slide the frittata onto a large round platter.

Add another tablespoon of olive oil to the same skillet and make the second fritatta. Then repeat the process and make the third fritatta.

Place slices of mozzarella cheese on top of the first fritatta. Then top with tomato slices and sprinkle with pepper. Add the second fritatta and repeat the cheese, tomato, and pepper topping. Then add the third fritatta and repeat the process. Garnish the layers of fritatte with fresh basil leaves. When ready to serve, cut the fritatte into large wedges like a pie.

SERVES 8

~ *Insalata di Tonno e Fagioli* ~
Tuna and Bean Salad

3 (15 ounce) cans cannellini beans,
   drained
1 cup coarsely chopped onion
1 (6½ ounce) can Italian tuna
   packed in oil, drained

5 tablespoons extra virgin olive oil
¼ teaspoon salt
½ teaspoon freshly ground black
   pepper

Place the cannellini beans in a large serving bowl and add the onions. Break the tuna apart with a fork and mix it with the beans and onions. Add the oil and season with the salt and freshly ground pepper. Mix well, cover the bowl, and place it in the refrigerator until ready to serve.

SERVES 8

~ *Torta di Limone con Noci* ~
Lemon Cake with Walnuts

¾ cup chopped walnuts
3 cups flour
½ teaspoon baking soda
½ teaspoon salt
1 cup milk
2 tablespoons lemon rind
½ teaspoon lemon extract

4 drops yellow food coloring
   (optional)
1 cup (2 sticks) unsalted butter, at
   room temperature
2 cups sugar
1 (3 ounce) package lemon gelatin
6 eggs, at room temperature

Place the chopped walnuts in the bottom of a 10-inch greased Bundt pan.
   Sift together the flour, baking soda, and salt. Stir together the milk, lemon rind, lemon extract, and food coloring in a small bowl.
   Cream the butter with an electric mixer in a large bowl. Gradually add the sugar and gelatin and beat for 5 minutes. Add the eggs one at a time, beating 1 minute after each addition. Scrape the bowl frequently. Reduce mixer speed to the lowest setting and add the flour mixture alternately with the milk mixture, beating well after each addition.
   Pour the batter into the prepared pan and level the top with a rubber spatula. Bake in a preheated 350° oven for about 1½ hours or

until a cake tester inserted in the center of the cake comes out clean. Remove the cake from the oven and cool on a rack for about 20 minutes. Then turn the cake out onto a serving plate. While the cake is still warm, poke holes in the top and pour the glaze over the top. Let the cake cool completely before serving. (If using a 10-inch tube pan, reduce the baking time by 10 to 15 minutes.)

LEMON GLAZE:

1½ cups powdered sugar   2 teaspoons grated lemon peel
2½ tablespoons lemon juice

Combine the powdered sugar, lemon juice, and lemon peel in a small bowl until well blended and spread over the top of the cake.

SERVES 8 to 12

Brunch Stile Italiano
Italian-Style Brunch

Sciampagna con Succo d'Arancia
Champagne with Orange Juice

Salsicce e Prosciutto con Polenta
Sausages and Ham with Polenta

Frittata di Patate
Potato Omelet

Asparagi con Limone
Asparagus with Lemon

Anguria Ripiena all'Amaretto
Stuffed Watermelon and Amaretto Liqueur

Caffè Espresso
Espresso

SERVES 6

In Italy there is no meal like the American brunch. Breakfast in Italy includes Caffè Latte, which is a very strong coffee served with lots of hot milk. Bread, butter, and some marmalade or jam accompany the coffee.

Brunch is an American phenomenon, a combination of breakfast and lunch, which is usually served on weekends. I have devised an Italian menu for this occasion that combines many of the elements usually served at a brunch—eggs, sausages, ham, and potatoes. The roasted polenta acts almost as a bread or a cornstick to accompany the sausages. The eggs in this menu are in the form of an omelet, which is known as a frittata in Italy. This frittata contains potatoes, which are also a nice addition to the meats. The Asparagus with Lemon adds a nice tangy flavor in contrast to the sausages and ham.

The melon-fruit dessert adds a light finishing touch to the brunch.

My Italian relatives, who are used to their plain breakfasts, always request that I cook this menu for them whenever I visit them in Italy or they visit me here.

Preparations

You might want to plan on serving this brunch late in the morning, since much of the preparation and cooking is done about an hour and a half before the guests arrive.

You can make the polenta on the day before the brunch. When it has cooled, wrap it in aluminum foil, and store it in the refrigerator. Also on the day before the brunch you will want to prepare the watermelon shell and make the melon balls, storing each separately, covered with plastic wrap, in the refrigerator. You can also clean the asparagus at this time.

On the morning of the brunch make the grapefruit-Amaretto sauce for the fruit. Then slice the pears, assemble the watermelon dessert, and refrigerate it until serving time. Also in the morning, cut the polenta into slices, place them on an oiled baking sheet, add Parmesan cheese, and set aside.

You can cook the asparagus and either keep it at room temperature or store it in the refrigerator until half an hour before serving so that it warms up. However, you may choose to steam it while the omelet is cooking. In any event, to avoid a last minute rush, make the dressing for the asparagus before starting the cooking.

One hour before your guests are expected, make the Potato Omelet and keep it warm in a 150° oven. A half hour before the doorbell is supposed to ring, fry the sausages and ham slices and also place them in the oven to keep warm.

Put the sliced polenta in the preheated oven just as your guests arrive. (If you do not have two ovens remove the omelet and the meats and cover them loosely with aluminum foil to keep warm. After you have removed the polenta you may want to put both back in the oven for a couple of minutes with the oven door open.)

Open the champagne and serve it with fresh orange juice.

~ *Sciampagna con Succo d'Arancia* ~
Champagne with Orange Juice

2 quarts freshly squeezed orange
   juice

2 bottles brut champagne

Pour equal parts of orange juice and champagne into large balloon-type champagne glasses. Serve preceding and accompanying the brunch.

SERVES 6

~ *Salsicce e Prosciutto con Polenta* ~
Sausages and Ham with Polenta

ROASTED POLENTA:

6 cups water
1½ teaspoons salt
1½ cups yellow cornmeal

6 tablespoons (¾ stick) butter, cut
   in pieces
3 tablespoons olive oil
Freshly grated Parmesan cheese

Bring the water to a boil in a large saucepan and add the salt. Gradually add the cornmeal in a thin stream and stir constantly with a wooden spoon until the mixture boils and thickens, about 2 minutes. Reduce the heat to low, add the butter, and continue stirring until the butter is melted and mixed with the cornmeal. Continue cooking the mixture over low heat until thick, stirring occasionally, about 30 minutes. The polenta is cooked when it comes away cleanly from the sides of the pot.

Remove it from the heat and pour the polenta onto a buttered cookie sheet. Let it cool and then remove it from the cookie sheet. (The polenta may be made to this point the day before, wrapped in aluminum foil and stored in the refrigerator.)

To roast the polenta, cut it into 2 by 5-inch pieces. Pour the olive oil onto a baking sheet and spread it evenly. Place the pieces of polenta on the baking sheet, turning them once to coat them with oil. Then sprinkle the cheese over them and bake in a preheated 400° oven for 30 minutes or until golden. Remove and place the pieces of polenta on a serving platter.

6 mild Italian sausages, casings   6 slices ham (1½ pounds)
   removed

Flatten the sausages slightly with a long spatula and fry them in a dry non-stick skillet over medium heat. Turn the sausages after 5 minutes and cook for another 5 minutes until browned. Place the sausages on a warm platter.

In the same skillet, using the drippings from the sausages, sauté the ham slices over medium heat until lightly browned, turning them once. Place the ham slices on the platter with the sausages and serve hot with the roasted polenta.

SERVES 6

~ Frittata di Patate ~
Potato Omelet

3 slices bacon, finely chopped
2 tablespoons olive oil
1 cup chopped onion
¼ cup chopped red bell pepper
¼ cup chopped green bell pepper
3 cups chopped potatoes
½ teaspoon salt

¼ teaspoon freshly ground black
   pepper
8 large eggs
¼ teaspoon salt
¼ teaspoon black pepper
1/8 teaspoon nutmeg
1/3 cup freshly grated Parmesan
   cheese

Sauté the bacon in the olive oil in a medium non-stick skillet over medium heat for 2 minutes. Add the onions, red and green peppers, and potatoes and continue cooking until the potato mixture starts to brown. Remove the skillet from heat and set aside.

Beat the eggs with salt, pepper, nutmeg, and Parmesan cheese in a medium bowl. Return the skillet to the heat and add the egg mixture, stir to combine, and smooth out the top. Cook, covered, over low heat for 10 minutes or until the eggs are almost set. Remove lid and place the skillet in the oven with the broiler preheated. Broil for 2 minutes, watching the omelet closely so that it does not burn. Slide the omelet onto a serving platter, cut into thick wedges, and serve.

SERVES 6

~ *Asparagi con Limone* ~
Asparagus with Lemon

2 pounds asparagus
Juice of 1 large lemon
¼ teaspoon salt

¼ teaspoon freshly ground black
    pepper
⅓ cup extra virgin olive oil

Trim the asparagus of any leaves below the tip and cut off the tough ends. Wash the asparagus in cold water and tie in two bunches with string or a rubber band.

Place the asparagus upright in an asparagus cooker or stock pot. Add 3 inches of cold, lightly salted water. Bring to a boil, cover, and cook over high heat for 4 to 6 minutes, depending on the thickness of the asparagus. Remove the string and place the asparagus on a platter lined with paper towels to drain. Then put in the refrigerator to cool.

Combine the lemon juice and salt and pepper in a small bowl and whisk in the oil until blended.

To serve, remove paper towels underneath the asparagus and pour the dressing over it.

SERVES 6

~ *Anguria Ripiena all'Amaretto* ~
Stuffed Watermelon and Amaretto Liqueur

1 watermelon (3½ to 5 pounds)
2 medium cantaloupes
3 pears
Juice of 2 pink grapefruits

2 tablespoons sugar
6 tablespoons Amaretto liqueur
8 to 10 mint leaves, for garnish

Cut top off watermelon. Take out the pulp with a melon baller and remove the seeds. With a spoon scrape the walls of the watermelon until smooth. Cut the top rim of the watermelon into zigzags for decoration and place the melon in the refrigerator until ready to fill.

Cut the cantaloupes in half, remove the seeds, and remove the flesh with a melon baller. Cut the pears, remove the core, and cut into slices. Place the fruit in the watermelon shell and mix gently.

Combine the grapefruit juice, sugar, and Amaretto liqueur in a bowl. Mix well and pour over the fruit. Decorate with mint leaves and refrigerate until ready to serve.

SERVES 6

Polenta con Gusto
Polenta with Taste

Polenta
Polenta

Coniglio con Olive Nere
Rabbit with Black Olives

Quaglie al Funghi
Quails with Mushrooms

Insalata con Pera e Formaggio
Salad with Pear and Cheese

Mele Cotte al Forno
Baked Apples

Caffè
Coffee

SERVES 6 to 8

Polenta, a porridge of coarse cornmeal, is a staple food of Italy and ranks in popularity with pasta and rice. Its history goes back to Roman times when it was made with various grains. It was not until corn from the New World came to northern Italy in the 16th century that polenta was made with cornmeal. At that time it was regarded as a dish for the poor and has often been thought of as peasant food to be eaten primarily in the winter. Today, however, polenta ranks in popularity with pasta and risotto in Northern Italy. It may be served with various sauces and with melted cheeses.

The majority of polenta is now made with yellow cornmeal, although white cornmeal is also used. Another version of it is made with "il grano saraceno," which is buckwheat flour.

Since polenta is an ideal base for various dishes and sauces, I decided to use two different entrées to accompany it. I use coarse-grained cornmeal for the polenta since that gives it a crunchier texture. Smoother grained cornmeals may also be used.

The pear and cheese salad is a refreshing one after the rich sauces of the rabbit and quail. Since sweet apples are often baked for dessert in Italy, I am using the flavorful Golden Delicious apple for the dessert for this polenta feast. It is baked in wine and garnished with nuts.

Preparations

If time permits, you should make both of the main dishes at least a day ahead so that the flavors of the sauces can be absorbed by the meats. Prepare the salad ingredients, with the exception of the pear, in the afternoon and store them in the refrigerator. Peel and cube the pear just before serving the salad. The dressing may also be made in the afternoon.

Late in the afternoon, prepare the apples, bake them, and reduce the sauce if necessary. They should be served warm or slightly above room temperature. If they are not warm enough slip the apples back in the oven while you are eating the salad.

~ *Polenta* ~

8 cups water
2 teaspoons salt
2 cups coarse-grained yellow

cornmeal
8 tablespoons (1 stick) butter, cut in
    pieces

Bring the water and salt to a boil in a heavy, large, deep saucepan. Gradually whisk in the cornmeal. Stir briskly with a wooden spoon until the mixture boils and thickens, about 2 minutes. Reduce the heat to low, add the butter and continue stirring briskly until it is melted and mixed with the polenta. Cook over low heat until thick, stirring occasionally, for about 30 minutes. The polenta is cooked when it comes away cleanly from the sides of the pot. Pour the polenta on a large wooden board or on a large platter and serve with a dish that has a sauce.

HINT: If you have leftover polenta, cut the cold polenta into 2-inch pieces and fry them in hot oil until lightly golden.

You may also cut the cold polenta into large slices and place them in a buttered baking dish. Top each slice with 1 slice of fontina cheese and bake in a preheated 350° oven until the cheese is melted. Place under a preheated broiler for a few seconds for a golden crust.

SERVES 8

~ *Coniglio con Olive Nere* ~
Rabbit with Black Olives

1 rabbit (3 to 3½ pounds)
4 tablespoons olive oil
1 tablespoon unsalted butter
½ onion, finely chopped
2 cloves garlic, finely chopped
1 tablespoon finely chopped fresh
    sage
1 tablespoon finely chopped fresh
    rosemary

2 tablespoons finely chopped fresh
    parsley
2 cups red wine
¼ teaspoon salt
¼ teaspoon freshly ground black
    pepper
1½ cups chicken broth
1 cup pitted black olives
1 cup tomato sauce

Remove all visible fat from the rabbit, cut it into pieces, rinse under cold water, and pat dry with a paper towel.

Place the olive oil and butter in a large flameproof casserole or deep skillet over medium heat. When the butter is bubbling, add the rabbit pieces and sauté until brown on one side. Turn the rabbit pieces and add the onion, garlic, sage, rosemary, and parsley and sauté on the other side until browned.

Add the wine and cook until it has evaporated. Season the rabbit with the salt and pepper and cook, over medium heat, for 30 minutes, occasionally adding some of the broth when the pan juices have cooked down. Use all of the broth.

Add the olives and the tomato sauce. Mix thoroughly and cook, covered, for 30 minutes over low heat, stirring occasionally. When cooked, transfer the rabbit pieces, the olives, and the sauce to a large preheated platter and serve with polenta.

SERVES 4 as a main course or 8 with another dish

~ Quaglie al Funghi ~
Quails with Mushrooms

1 ounce dried porcini mushrooms
8 quails
Salt
Freshly ground black pepper
8 slices pancetta or bacon
¾ pound fresh mushrooms

6 tablespoons (¾ stick) unsalted
    butter
1 tablespoon extra virgin olive oil
2 cloves garlic, peeled
½ cup brandy
2 cups chicken broth
2 tablespoons chopped fresh parsley

Soak the porcini mushrooms in 2 cups of warm water for 20 minutes. Remove them from the water and chop them coarsely. (Strain the water and reserve for another use such as soup stocks.)

Wash the quails and pat them dry with paper towels inside and out. Sprinkle salt and pepper inside the cavities and on the outside of the birds. Place one slice pancetta over each quail breast and secure it with a toothpick or a string.

Heat 3 tablespoons butter and the oil in a skillet over medium heat. When the butter is hot, add the garlic, the fresh sliced mushrooms, and the porcini mushrooms and sauté until all of the liquid has evaporated.

Heat the remaining 3 tablespoons butter in a large, heavy flameproof casserole or ovenproof skillet over medium-high heat. When the foam subsides, add the quails and brown them on all sides. Pour the brandy over the quails and let the liquid evaporate for a few minutes. Then add the broth and the sautéed mushrooms. Bring to a boil, and cook, covered, over low heat for about 25 minutes, turning the birds occasionally. Then uncover the casserole, remove the bacon, and place the casserole in a preheated 350° oven to allow the quail breasts to brown.

Remove excess grease from the casserole drippings and arrange the quails, mushrooms, and sauce on a hot serving platter. Sprinkle parsley over the top. If the sauce is too thin, thicken with 2 tablespoons of butter rubbed together with 2 tablespoons of flour and whisk into the hot sauce, simmering until thickened.

SERVES 4 as a main course or 8 with another dish

~ *Insalata con Pera e Formaggio* ~
Salad with Pear and Cheese

1 large head butter lettuce
1 medium head radicchio
1 medium Belgian endive
1 cup cubed fontina cheese
¼ cup slivered Parmesan cheese
⅓ cup chopped walnuts

1 pear, peeled and cut in pieces
⅓ cup olive oil
Juice of 1 lemon
¼ teaspoon salt
¼ teaspoon freshly ground black
   pepper

Wash and spin dry the lettuces, break them in pieces, and place them in a large salad bowl. Add the cubes of fontina cheese, Parmesan slivers, walnuts and, just before serving, the pear pieces. Make the salad dressing by mixing the oil with the lemon juice, salt, and pepper and pour over the salad and toss until well blended.

SERVES 8

~ *Mele Cotte al Forno* ~
Baked Apples

8 large Golden Delicious apples
½ cup sugar
4 tablespoons (½ stick) unsalted
   butter
½ cup pine nuts

½ cup sliced almonds
½ cup white wine
⅔ cup water
Powdered sugar, for garnish

Peel and core the apples. Place 1 tablespoon sugar and ½ tablespoon butter in each of the cored apples. Butter a baking dish and combine the pine nuts and almonds in the bottom of the dish. Place the apples on top of the nuts. Combine the wine and water and pour over the apples. Bake in a preheated 350° oven for 40 to 50 minutes, basting the apples occasionally with the juices.

Place the baked apples on a serving dish or on individual plates. Reduce the juice in a small saucepan until it turns caramel color. Then spoon the syrup along with the nuts over the apples. Sprinkle with powdered sugar and serve either hot or warm.

SERVES 8

Una Festa di Caccia
A Hunter's Feast

Risotto con Ragù di Quaglie
Risotto with Quail Sauce

Fagiano con Olive Verdi
Pheasant with Green Olives

Petti di Fargiani Fritti
Fried Breast of Pheasant

Tortore con Porcini
Doves with Porcini Mushrooms

Insalata Mista all'Arancia
Mixed Salad with Orange

Torta di Castagne con Cioccolata Glassa
Chestnut Cake with Chocolate Glaze

Caffè Espresso
Espresso

SERVES 6 to 8

Since there are numerous forests in Northern Italy, game, particularly birds, are abundant and are hunted. Game of all types is also available in the markets there. In this country it is possible to purchase domestically raised game birds from specialty growers. However, there are many hunters, such as my husband, who enjoy the sport and bring home the game to be cooked.

For this grand hunter's feast I have chosen to prepare a Risotto with Quail Sauce, two dishes with pheasant, and Doves with Porcini Mushrooms. The risotto is a mild dish and balances the delicate flavors of the doves. The legs and thighs of the pheasant are braised, and the breast is quickly fried so as not to dry out the meat. The doves are complemented with the flavor of the porcini mushrooms and are braised in a wine and brandy sauce.

Any of the smaller birds of similar size, such as guinea hen, grouse, ptarmigan, sage hen, or partridge may be substituted for the pheasant. However, since they are smaller birds you will want to use the entire bird in the first recipe and eliminate frying the breast of the birds. Squabs, quail, or woodcocks may be substituted for the doves.

A refreshing salad offers a pleasant interlude before a traditional Italian chestnut torte for dessert. This cake is usually prepared during the fall which is also hunting season.

Preparations

The quail sauce for the risotto can be made in the morning or early afternoon and set aside. Then before the dinner you can warm the sauce, mix it with the rice, and proceed to finish the risotto.

You will find that if you make the Pheasant with Green Olives and the Doves with Porcini Mushrooms in the morning, or better yet, the day before, the game will better absorb the flavors of the sauces. Then you can warm the two dishes just before serving. The breasts of pheasant, however, should be fried just before you serve the risotto. They can be kept warm in a 150° oven.

If you so desire, clean and tear the lettuce in the morning, place it in a plastic bag, and refrigerate until ready to assemble the salad. Just before your guests arrive, cut the orange and make the dressing. Toss the salad just before serving.

Depending on your time schedule, the chestnut cake can be made either the day before or on the morning of your party. In either case, prepare the chestnuts ahead. They will keep at room temperature.

~ *Risotto con Ragù di Quaglie* ~
Risotto with Quail Sauce

8 quails
8 large fresh sage leaves, chopped
8 small fresh rosemary sprigs,
    chopped
¼ cup chopped fresh parsley
3 cloves garlic, peeled and cut in
    slices
¼ teaspoon salt
¼ teaspoon freshly ground black
    pepper
¼ cup flour
6 tablespoons (¾ stick) butter

3 tablespoons olive oil
¹/₃ cup gin
½ cup dry white wine
½ cup Marsala wine
1 tablespoon tomato paste diluted
    with 2 tablespoons warm water
1 onion, finely chopped
4 cups chicken broth
2 cups Italian Arborio rice
¹/₃ cup freshly grated Parmesan
    cheese

Rinse the quails and pat them dry inside and out. Place some of the sage, rosemary, parsley, and garlic inside each quail. Season the birds with salt and pepper and roll them in the flour.

Heat 2 tablespoons of the butter and the oil in a skillet over medium-high heat, and when hot, add the quails. Cook over medium heat until the quails are roasted and brown.

Sprinkle the gin over the birds and let it evaporate. Then add the wine, Marsala, and diluted tomato paste. Cover the skillet and cook over medium heat for 40 to 45 minutes, depending on the size and age of the quails.

When the quails are cooked, remove them from the skillet. When cooled, remove the skin and the bones, and chop the meat. Place the meat back in the sauce and simmer together for 3 minutes. If the sauce is too dry, add a few spoonfuls of hot water. Keep the quail sauce warm while cooking the rice.

Bring the chicken broth to a simmer in a saucepan. Sauté the onion in 2 tablespoons of the butter in a large saucepan over medium heat. When the onion is limp, add the hot broth. Bring the broth to a boil, add the rice, and mix well. When the mixture boils again, cover the saucepan, reduce the heat to low, and cook for 15 minutes or until the rice is done but al dente. Remove the saucepan from the heat. Add the remaining 2 tablespoons butter and the Parmesan cheese to the rice. Mix thoroughly, then add the quail sauce and mix thoroughly again. Serve immediately while hot.

SERVES 6 to 8

~ *Fagiano con Olive Verdi* ~
Pheasant with Green Olives

8 pheasant legs and thighs
3 tablespoons butter, unsalted
1/3 cup olive oil
2 slices pancetta or bacon, chopped
1 onion, chopped
1 celery stalk, chopped
1 small carrot, finely chopped
2 cloves garlic, chopped
3 tablespoons chopped fresh parsley
1/2 teaspoon chopped fresh marjoram

1/2 teaspoon salt
1/2 teaspoon freshly ground black
    pepper
1 cup dry white wine
1 cup chicken broth
1 (14 1/2 ounce) can peeled Italian
    tomatoes with juice, tomatoes
    chopped
1 cup green olives with pits,
    drained

Rinse and pat the pheasant legs and thighs dry.

Place the butter and the olive oil in a large saucepan or Dutch oven over medium-high heat, and when hot, add the pancetta, onion, celery, carrot, garlic, parsley, and marjoram. Sauté over medium heat until the vegetables are limp, about 10 minutes. Add the pheasant pieces to the pan and cook, turning them over, until all the pieces are golden on both sides. Season with the salt and pepper.

Add the white wine and let it evaporate over high heat. Then add the chicken broth and the chopped tomatoes with the juice. Mix thoroughly, reduce the heat to low, cover, and cook slowly, stirring occasionally, for about 50 to 60 minutes. (The cooking time will vary depending on the age and size of the pheasant. Make a small cut in the thigh to see if the meat is done. If not done and the sauce is too dense, add more broth and continue cooking.)

After 30 minutes of cooking, add the green olives and continue cooking until the pheasant is done. Place the cooked pheasant on a large preheated platter, add the olives, and pour the sauce over it. Serve hot.

SERVES 6 to 8

~ Petti di Fargiani Fritti ~
Fried Breast of Pheasant

4 pheasant breasts, skinned, boned,
   and split in half
2 eggs, beaten
¾ cup bread crumbs

¼ cup freshly grated Parmesan
   cheese
Salt and pepper, to taste
¼ cup olive oil
½ cup dry white wine

Rinse and pat the pheasant breasts dry. Beat the eggs in a shallow bowl. Combine the bread crumbs, Parmesan cheese, salt, and pepper on a piece of waxed paper or aluminum foil.

Dip the pheasant breasts in the beaten egg and then in the bread crumb mixture, pressing down on the meat to adhere the crumbs.

Heat the oil in a large sauté pan over medium-high heat. When hot, add the pheasant and sauté over medium heat until golden brown on both sides. Remove the pheasant breasts to a warmed platter. Add the wine to the pan and cook for a few minutes. Then return the meat for a minute or two to absorb the juices. Serve hot.

SERVES 6 to 8

~ Tortore con Porcini ~
Doves with Porcini Mushrooms

1 cup dried porcini mushrooms
12 doves
Salt and freshly ground black pepper
6 bacon slices, cut in half
2 tablespoons butter
3 tablespoons olive oil
1 tablespoon chopped fresh sage
1 tablespoon chopped fresh
   rosemary

4 tablespoon chopped fresh parsley
3 medium cloves garlic, finely
   chopped
1 medium onion, finely chopped
½ cup dry white wine
¼ cup brandy
1 cup chicken broth
1 cup liquid from the soaked porcini

Soak the porcini mushrooms in a small bowl in 1½ cups of hot water for 15 minutes. Remove the mushrooms and strain the liquid through a fine sieve. Reserve the mushroom liquid for later use. Rinse the mushrooms under cold running water, drain, and chop.

Rinse the doves and pat them dry inside and out. Sprinkle them with salt and pepper inside and out. Place a half slice of bacon around each dove and secure it with a wooden toothpick or use white thread to tie it.

Place the butter and oil in a large saucepan or Dutch oven over medium heat and when the butter has melted, add the doves. Sauté them over medium heat, for about 20 minutes, or until the doves begin to turn brown, turning them often. Add the sage, rosemary, parsley, garlic, and onion and sauté for a couple more minutes. Add the wine and brandy and let evaporate. Then add the chicken broth and 1 cup of liquid from the soaked porcini. Cover the pan and cook, over moderate heat, for 15 to 20 minutes turning the doves often. (The cooking time varies depending on the size and age of the doves. They should be cooked but not overcooked so that they fall apart.) After 10 minutes of cooking, add the chopped porcini to the doves.

When the doves are ready, remove the bacon pieces and the toothpicks or thread. Place the doves on a preheated platter and pour the sauce over them. Serve hot.

This dish may be prepared several days ahead. The more the birds soak in the sauce, the better they are.

SERVES 6 to 8

~ *Insalata Mista all'Arancia* ~
Mixed Salad with Orange

1 celery heart (3 to 4 stalks),
*   julienned*
1 head butter lettuce, cut into strips
2 small heads or 1 medium head
*   radicchio, cut into strips*
1 orange

Juice of ½ lemon
¼ cup extra virgin olive oil
¼ teaspoon salt
¼ teaspoon freshly ground black
*   pepper*

Place the celery, lettuce, and radicchio in a large salad bowl. Cut the orange in half. Cut half of the orange into thin slices and reserve to place around the edges of the salad bowl for decoration.

Squeeze the juice from the other half of the orange into a small bowl and add the juice from the lemon, the olive oil, salt, and pepper and whisk until well blended. Pour the dressing over the salad, toss and serve.

SERVES 6 to 8

~ *Torta di Castagne con Cioccolata Glassa* ~
Chestnut Cake with Chocolate Glaze

1 pound fresh chestnuts
5 ounces slivered almonds, coarsely
chopped
5 large eggs, separated

1¼ cups sugar
8 tablespoons (1 stick) butter, cut
into pieces, at room temperature
2 tablespoons grated lemon rind

Grease and lightly flour a 9-inch springform pan.

Cut the chestnuts in half vertically and place them in a saucepan with sufficient water to cover them. Bring to a boil over high heat and continue to boil over medium high heat for 10 minutes. Drain the chestnuts until cool enough to handle, about 5 minutes. With the aid of a paring knife remove the shells and brown skin. (They will almost pop out of the skin.)

Purée the chestnuts in the bowl of a food processor. Combine the chestnut purée and the almonds in a bowl. Beat the egg yolks with an electric mixer until thick and lemon colored, about 10 minutes. Add the sugar and beat until smooth. With the mixer at low speed, blend in the softened butter, lemon rind, and chestnut mixture. Then beat until a smooth and light texture is formed.

Beat the egg whites until stiff and gently fold them into the egg mixture. Carefully pour the batter into the prepared pan and bake in a preheated 350° oven for 35 to 40 minutes or until a cake tester inserted in the center comes out clean. Cool the cake on a wire rack, then remove it from the pan and glaze the cake. Cut into wedges and serve.

CHOCOLATE GLAZE:

5 tablespoons butter
3 tablespoons superfine sugar

4 tablespoons brandy
5 ounces semisweet chocolate, grated

Bring the butter, sugar, and brandy to a boil over medium heat. Remove the pan from the heat and add the chocolate, stirring constantly until the chocolate is melted. Gently pour the glaze over the cake. Some of the glaze will run down the sides.

SERVES 8

Un Pranzo per la Promessa Sposa
A Bridal Luncheon

Aperitivo di Sciampagna
Champagne Aperitif

Riso e Piselli
Rice with Peas

Petti di Pollo Ripieni
Stuffed Chicken Breasts

Insalata di Indivia e Radicchio
Salad of Belgian Endive and Radicchio

Sorbetto di Fragole
Strawberry Sorbet

Caffè
Coffee

SERVES 6

The prospect of a wedding is a happy occasion and calls for a toast of champagne. I decided to add some orange juice and apricot brandy to champagne to make this special aperitif.

If your bridal luncheon is being held when the weather is warm, you may want to serve it outside. In the spring and summer, many luncheons, especially festive ones, are served in the garden in Italian homes. Flowers abound and birds add their song to greet the bride and her friends.

Preparations

Although much of the preparation for this luncheon is done in the morning, you will find that it is an easy meal to prepare. The salad ingredients can be prepared the night before, placed in plastic bags, and stored in the refrigerator. The Strawberry Sorbet should be

made about 24 hours in advance of the party, but not too mu[...]
ther ahead since it may tend to become icy. You can also she[...]
peas for the rice the day before.

You will want to prepare the chicken first since it takes longest.
Then you can make the rice dish while the chicken is cooking. If you
desire, you may want to serve small dinner rolls or slices of French
baguettes with both the chicken and the salad course. The Biscotti
cookies (for recipe see page 147), which are served with the Strawberry Sorbet, can be baked a day or two ahead.

...itivo di Sciampagna ~
...hampagne Aperitif

1½ ounces apricot brandy

Mix the champag... orange juice, and brandy together. Serve well chilled.

SERVES 6

~ *Riso e Piselli* ~
Rice with Peas

4¼ cups homemade chicken broth
4 tablespoons (½ stick) unsalted
  butter
1 tablespoon olive oil
3 slices lean pancetta or bacon,
  diced
1 onion, chopped
3 cups shelled fresh green peas

¼ teaspoon salt
¼ teaspoon freshly ground black
  pepper
2 cups Italian Arborio rice
½ cup freshly grated Parmesan
  cheese
1 tablespoon chopped fresh parsley

Bring the broth barely to a simmer.

Heat three tablespoons of the butter and oil together in a large saucepan over medium heat. Sauté the pancetta or bacon and onion until both turn a golden brown. Add the fresh peas and ¼ cup of the chicken broth. Cook for about 10 minutes over low heat; then season with the salt and pepper. Add the rest of the simmering broth and bring the mixture back to a boil. Pour in the rice and stir well. Reduce the heat to low and cook covered for 15 minutes.

The rice is done when it is tender and cooked through but still firm to the bite. When the rice is done, stir in the remaining tablespoon of butter and the grated cheese. Mix thoroughly, sprinkle with chopped parsley, and serve either on individual plates or from a warm platter.

SERVES 6

~ *Petti di Pollo Ripieni* ~
Stuffed Chicken Breasts

3 whole chicken breasts, cut in half, skinned, and deboned
6 thin slices prosciutto or boiled ham
6 slices fontina cheese
6 fresh sage leaves
½ cup milk
½ cup flour

4 tablespoons (½ stick) unsalted butter
½ cup chicken broth
1 cup dry white wine
¼ teaspoon salt
¼ teaspoon freshly ground black pepper
⅓ cup whipping cream

Flatten the chicken breasts with a mallet until the meat is of uniform thickness. Place 1 slice of prosciutto or boiled ham, 1 slice of fontina cheese, and 1 sage leaf on each piece of chicken breast. Roll up the chicken breast and secure it with a toothpick. Dip the chicken breasts in milk and then roll them in flour, coating each piece completely.

Melt the butter in a large skillet over medium heat and when the butter foams, add the chicken breasts. Sauté over medium heat, turning the chicken until golden on all sides.

Add the chicken broth and ½ cup of the wine to the skillet. Season with salt and pepper and continue cooking until the liquid has been reduced by half; then add the remaining wine. Cover the skillet and simmer for 15 minutes on low heat, turning the chicken breasts occasionally. If the sauce looks too dry, add a little more broth.

Place the chicken breasts on a warm platter. Increase the heat and add the cream to the skillet, mixing well, and scraping up any brown particles. Adjust seasonings, if necessary. Spoon the sauce over the chicken breasts and serve.

SERVES 6

~ *Insalata di Indivia e Radicchio* ~
Salad of Belgian Endive and Radicchio

2 medium heads radicchio
2 medium heads Belgian endive
1 large bunch arugula
5 tablespoons extra virgin olive oil

Juice of one lemon
½ teaspoon salt
½ teaspoon freshly ground black
 pepper

Wash and dry all of the salad ingredients. Cut the endive and radicchio into ½-inch wide strips and mix with the arugula in a large salad bowl. Make the dressing by mixing together the olive oil and lemon juice and season with the salt and pepper. Pour the dressing over the salad just before serving.

SERVES 6

~ *Sorbetto di Fragole* ~
Strawberry Sorbet

½ cup red wine
1 cup sugar
2 tablespoons lemon juice
½ cup orange juice

3 pints fresh strawberries (about
 6 cups)
Strawberries, for garnish
Mint leaves, for garnish

Combine the wine, sugar, and lemon and orange juices in a noncorrosive pan and boil for 5 minutes; cool. Purée the strawberries in a blender or food processor and add them to the cooled syrup. Pour the mixture into a container, cover it with aluminum foil, and freeze for approximately 6 hours or until it is slushy.

Remove the sorbet from the freezer and beat it until it is fluffy. Return to freezer and freeze overnight.

Twenty minutes before serving, remove the sorbet from the freezer and place it in the refrigerator. Spoon the sorbet into individual glass dishes and garnish with whole fresh strawberries and mint leaves. Serve with a platter of Biscotti (see recipe on page 147).

SERVES 6 to 8

Un Pranzo per le Laureate
A Luncheon for the Graduates

Insalata di Radicchio, Funghi e Bresaola
Salad of Radicchio, Mushrooms, and Bresaola

Fusilli con Zucchine
Fusilli with Zucchini

Pesche al Vino Rosso
Peaches in Red Wine

Caffè
Coffee

SERVES 6

In Italy and the United States, graduation from school signifies the beginning of a new life, whether it is on to another institution of higher learning or entering the business world. It is a time when family and friends gather to honor the graduate.

Since most graduations take place when the weather is warm, I have chosen a light menu for this luncheon. It takes advantage of the fresh zucchini in the market and the first of the fresh peaches available.

A salad of radicchio, mushrooms, and bresaola starts this festive occasion. The slightly spicy saltiness of the bresaola is a pleasing contrast to the lightly bitter taste of the radicchio. Bresaola, a salt-cured and air-dried beef, is available in Italian markets as well as many gourmet shops and supermarkets. It is a speciality of the Lombardy region and for centuries has been served as an antipasto at important occasions. If bresaola is not available, prosciutto may be substituted.

Preparations

Many of the preparations for this simple luncheon can be done ahead. The last minute tasks are simple ones and not very time con-suming. On the morning of your luncheon you can wash the radic-chio, clean the mushrooms but not slice them, and cut the Parmesan cheese into slivers.

If you want to prepare part of the sauce for the Fusilli with Zuc-chini ahead, you can do so including the addition of the tomatoes. Just before serving, cook the pasta and finish cooking the sauce.

Prepare the peach dessert several hours before you plan to serve it so that the peaches can absorb the wine flavor. The accompanying Amaretti macaroons come in various sizes and are available in Italian groceries as well as many supermarkets.

~ *Insalata di Radicchio, Funghi e Bresaola* ~
Salad of Radicchio, Mushrooms, and Bresaola

1 medium head radicchio (about ½
    pound)
¼ pound small fresh mushrooms
12 very thin slices bresaola or
    prosciutto
¼ cup extra virgin olive oil

1 tablespoon wine vinegar
½ teaspoon salt
½ teaspoon freshly ground black
    pepper
1 cup slivered Parmesan cheese

Cut the head of radicchio in half. Remove the leaves, rinse them under cold water, and pat dry with paper towels. Clean the mushrooms and slice them thinly.

To serve, arrange 2 or 3 leaves of radicchio, depending on their size, on each salad plate. Place sliced mushrooms on the radicchio and top with 2 slices of bresaola.

Mix the olive oil, vinegar, salt, and pepper until well blended and pour the dressing over the salad. Sprinkle with slivers of Parmesan cheese and serve with small slices of French bread.

SERVES 6

~ *Fusilli con Zucchine* ~
Fusilli with Zucchini

2 tablespoons olive oil
2 tablespoons unsalted butter
2 cloves garlic, chopped
1 medium onion, chopped
4 ounces pancetta, cut in small
    cubes
1 pound zucchini, cut in slices
4 ounces zucchini flowers (12 to 14
    flowers), cut in strips (optional)
2 tablespoons chopped fresh parsley

½ cup dry white wine
½ teaspoon salt
½ teaspoon freshly ground black
    pepper
1 (14½ ounce) can Italian peeled
    tomatoes with juice, tomatoes
    chopped
1 pound fusilli
½ cup freshly grated Parmesan
    cheese

Choose a large heavy skillet that will later accommodate all of the zucchini. Put the oil and butter in the skillet and when the butter starts to foam add the garlic, onion, and pancetta. Sauté over medium heat until the onion is limp, then add the sliced zucchini and mix thoroughly. Continue cooking and stirring for a couple of minutes over medium heat. Add the optional zucchini flowers and parsley to the skillet and mix. Then add the wine and continue cooking until the wine has evaporated.

Season with the salt and pepper and add the chopped tomatoes and their juices. Mix thoroughly and cook uncovered until the zucchini is tender but still al dente. In the meantime, cook the fusilli until al dente and drain.

Place the pasta in a large serving bowl or on a platter, add the zucchini mixture, sprinkle with Parmesan cheese, toss thoroughly, and serve immediately.

SERVES 6 to 8

~ *Pesche al Vino Rosso* ~
Peaches in Red Wine

6 ripe, firm peaches   *3 cups dry red wine*
6 teaspoons sugar   *Amaretti macaroons*

Cut the peaches in half, remove the stones, and cut them into thick slices. Place the peaches in a deep bowl and sprinkle them with the sugar. Pour the wine over the peaches, cover the bowl, and set it aside for a few hours so that the peaches can absorb some of the wine. Do not refrigerate.

To serve, divide the peaches among six wide-stemmed glasses. Spoon the wine-juices over the peaches. Serve Amaretti macaroons as an accompaniment.

SERVES 6

Una Cena di Famiglia
A Family Dinner

Risotto con Radicchio Rosso
Risotto with Red Radicchio

Costolette di Maiale con Prosciutto
Stuffed Pork Chops with Prosciutto

Broccoli Rosolati
Sautéed Broccoli

Torta di Cioccolata
Chocolate Cake

Caffè Espresso
Espresso

SERVES 6

Italian family dinners are joyous occasions when food and wine are enjoyed. To me they are also an opportunity to serve many different dishes that various members of my family enjoy. I try to plan the menus of my family dinners around the availability of seasonal ingredients and the food preferences of my family.

For this menu I have chosen some of the favorites I serve to my Italian relatives when they come for a visit. The Risotto with Radicchio is an unusual one, which is not only colorful but very tasty. Traditional pork chops stuffed with prosciutto and cheese are served with Sautéed Broccoli. For dessert there is a Chocolate Cake accompanied by a very smooth Mascarpone Cream. We have many family dinners at our house with many different recipes.

Preparations

You may do most of the preparations for this dinner in the afternoon and then finish the cooking just before dinner. The risotto can be made up to the point of adding the rice. Simmer the broth later just before adding the rice. You can set the cooked vegetables aside and finish cooking the risotto about 25 minutes before dinner.

The pork chops can be stuffed early in the afternoon and refrigerated. If you want to cook them an hour or so ahead, you can do so up to the point of adding the Marsala. You can also prepare the broccoli and boil it early in the afternoon. However, after boiling the broccoli, immediately immerse it in cold water to stop the cooking process. Just before dinner sauté the broccoli with the garlic and parsley.

The Chocolate Cake and Mascarpone Velvet Cream may be made a day ahead.

~ Risotto con Radicch
Risotto with Red Ra(

¾ to 1 pound red radicchio
5 tablespoons unsalted butter
1 tablespoon olive oil
3 ounces pancetta or bacon, finely
    diced
½ medium onion, finely chopped
4¼ cups beef broth

½ cup (
2 cups
⅔ cup
    cheese
Salt and freshly ground black
    pepper, to taste

Wash the radicchio leaves in cold water, drain, and pat them dry with paper towels. Cut the leaves into thin strips about ¼ inch wide.

Place 3 tablespoons of the butter and the olive oil in a heavy-bottomed saucepan over medium heat. When the butter starts to foam, add the diced pancetta and chopped onion and sauté for about 5 minutes. While the pancetta and onion are cooking, place the broth in a saucepan and bring it to a low simmer. When the onion is limp, add the radicchio and cook, stirring occasionally, until the radicchio is tender and limp. Add the wine, stir, and let the wine evaporate for a few minutes.

Add the rice to the saucepan and stir to coat it with the pan juices. Add the hot broth, stir, and when the broth is boiling, cover the saucepan. Reduce the heat to low and cook slowly for about 17 minutes. The rice is done when it is cooked through but still al dente.

Remove the saucepan from the heat, stir in the remaining 2 tablespoons of butter and the Parmesan cheese, and mix thoroughly. Season with salt and pepper, stir, and serve at once.

SERVES 6

~ Costolette di Maiale con Prosciutto ~
Stuffed Pork Chops with Prosciutto

6 pork chops, about 1 inch thick
6 thin slices prosciutto
6 thin slices fontina cheese
2 large eggs
¼ teaspoon salt
¼ teaspoon freshly ground black
   pepper

1½ cups dry bread crumbs
4 tablespoons (½ stick) unsalted
   butter
4 tablespoons olive oil
¾ to 1 cup dry Marsala wine or
   sherry

Cut a horizontal slit as far as the bone in each chop or have your butcher cut it. Fill each chop with one slice of prosciutto and one slice of fontina cheese. Fasten the opening of each chop with 2 round wooden toothpicks.

Beat the eggs with the salt and pepper in a medium bowl. Spread the bread crumbs on aluminum foil. Dip each chop into the beaten eggs, then coat with bread crumbs. Use the palm of your hand to press the bread crumbs into the chops.

Place 3 tablespoons of the butter and the oil in a sauté pan large enough to accommodate all the chops. Melt the butter over medium-high heat and when the foam starts to subside, add the pork chops. Cook the chops 3 to 5 minutes on each side or until golden brown. Add the Marsala or sherry and stir well. Reduce the heat to low and cover the pan. Simmer slowly for 20 to 25 minutes or until the chops are tender.

Place the chops on a preheated serving platter and remove the toothpicks. Add the remaining tablespoon of butter to the pan, stirring and scraping the bottom of the pan with a wooden spoon to loosen any particles. Pour the sauce over the chops and serve immediately.

SERVES 6

~ *Broccoli Rosolati* ~
Sautéed Broccoli

2 pounds fresh broccoli
¼ cup extra virgin olive oil
2 cloves garlic, finely chopped
¼ teaspoon salt

¼ teaspoon freshly ground black
   pepper
3 tablespoons chopped fresh parsley

Trim the tough parts of the broccoli. Remove the outer leaves, peel the stems and cut them into pieces. Divide the tops into flowerets, rinse, and drain well.

Bring enough water to barely cover the broccoli to a boil in a large saucepan. Add the broccoli, cover, and reduce the heat. Simmer for 3 to 5 minutes, or until the stalks are tender. Drain thoroughly on paper towels.

Heat the oil in a large sauté skillet. Stir in the garlic and drained broccoli. Season with salt and pepper and add the chopped parsley. Cook over medium heat for 3 to 5 minutes, occasionally stirring gently. Place the broccoli on a preheated platter and pour the pan juices over it. Serve immediately with the stuffed pork chops.

SERVES 6

~ *Torta di Cioccolata* ~
Chocolate Cake

1 tablespoon unsalted butter, to
   grease pan
8 ounces semisweet chocolate,
   grated fine
4 tablespoons flour

4 eggs, separated
½ pound (2 sticks) unsalted butter,
   at room temperature
¾ cup sugar
¼ teaspoon salt

Butter the bottom of an 8-inch round cake pan, cover the bottom with wax paper, and butter the paper.

Combine the grated chocolate and flour in a bowl, mix well, and set aside. Beat the egg whites until peaks form and set them aside.

Place the butter, sugar, and egg yolks in a large mixing bowl. Beat the mixture, either by hand or with an electric mixer, until it is completely blended and smooth. Then add the salt and continue beating until the mixture is thick. Add the flour mixture to the yolk mixture, a little at a time, until completely blended. Then fold in the egg whites.

Pour the batter into the greased pan and smooth the surface with a spatula. Bake in the center of a preheated 350° oven for 45 to 50 minutes. The center of the cake should be moist and almost creamy. Let the cake cool before removing it from the pan.

Cut the cake into thick slices and serve with Mascarpone Velvet Cream.

CREMA DI MASCARPONE VELLUTATA:
MASCARPONE VELVET CREAM

1 pound mascarpone cheese (or
   cream cheese), at room temperature
½ cup sugar

4 egg yolks, beaten
2 tablespoons whipping cream
2 tablespoons cognac
Cocoa powder, for garnish

Cream the cheese in an electric blender or food processor or with an electric mixer until very smooth. Beat in the sugar, egg yolks, cream, and cognac, beating until very smooth and thick. Pour into a serving dish and chill. Sprinkle cocoa powder over the top before serving.

SERVES 8

Festa delle Mamma
Mother's Day Feast

Antipasto di Prosciutto e Carpaccio
Prosciutto and Carpaccio Appetizer

Penne con Salsicce e Crema
Penne with Sausages and Cream

Costolette di Vitello Ripiene
Stuffed Veal Chops

Pomodori Fritti
Fried Tomatoes

Mousse di Pesca
Peach Mousse

Caffè Espresso
Espresso

SERVES 6

Although Mother's Day comes only once a year, to me it is a wonderful experience to prepare a special dinner for mother, regardless of the day of the year. I learned to cook from my mother and have used some of her recipes throughout the years. This menu is typical of some of the dishes of my native area of Northern Italy.

The antipasto of prosciutto and carpaccio is reminiscent of special occasions. The Penne with Sausages and Cream provides a light first course for this special meal. Stuffed Veal Chops are served with Fried Tomatoes for an elegant entrée. A refreshing, smooth, light Peach Mousse ends this festive Mother's Day Feast.

Preparations

Much of the preparation for cooking can be done ahead for this meal, but there are last-minute tasks, so be sure to allow time for them. The antipasto of prosciutto and carpaccio should be assembled just before the guests arrive. However, the onion used in the dish may be chopped ahead.

You will find that the sausage and cream sauce for the penne is best if made just before your family is to arrive. The sauce is quick to make and even quicker if you chop the onion and tomatoes earlier in the day. Stuff the veal chops early in the afternoon. You can also sauté them in mid-afternoon, place them in a large ovenproof dish, and set them aside. Then you can further advance your preparations by making the sauce for the veal chops, sautéing the mushrooms, and setting both aside.

In the morning or early afternoon, take some time to wash and cut the tomatoes, wrap them in paper towels, and refrigerate. That evening fry the tomatoes and finish cooking the stuffed veal chops.

The Peach Mousse should be made the day before with 1 cup of the sliced peaches and frozen. Remove the mousse from the freezer at least a half hour before serving to let it soften. Slice and marinate the remaining peaches about an hour before the guests arrive.

~ *Antipasto di Prosciutto e Carpaccio* ~
Prosciutto and Carpaccio Appetizer

1 pound beef fillet, fat removed, and
   cut in thin slices
1 onion, finely chopped
2 tablespoons capers, drained

24 slivers Parmesan cheese
6 tablespoons extra virgin olive oil
Freshly ground black pepper
1 lemon, cut in wedges

Divide the beef slices into 6 equal portions. Place 2 slices of prosciutto to one side of each of 6 appetizer plates. Place one of the portions of sliced beef opposite the prosciutto on each plate. Sprinkle some onion, capers, and Parmesan cheese over each plate. Pour 1 tablespoon olive oil over the beef and top with freshly ground pepper. Serve each antipasto with a lemon wedge.

SERVES 6

~ *Penne con Salsicce e Crema* ~
Penne with Sausages and Cream

6 tablespoons (¾ stick) unsalted
   butter
½ medium onion, finely chopped
½ pound mild Italian sausages,
   casings removed, crumbled
½ cup dry white wine
1½ cups whipping cream
Salt

¼ teaspoon freshly ground black
   pepper
¼ teaspoon nutmeg
1 cup chopped fresh tomatoes, peeled,
   seeded, and cut in small pieces
1 pound penne
½ cup freshly grated Parmesan
   cheese

Melt the butter in a large skillet over low heat and sauté the onion and the crumbled sausages for 7 to 10 minutes. Add the white wine and raise the heat to medium. When the wine has evaporated, add the cream and stir until the cream has thickened. Do not boil the cream. Season with salt (very little if the sausage is salty), pepper, and nutmeg, and add the fresh tomato pieces. Mix thoroughly and keep warm.

Cook the pasta until it is al dente, drain, add it to the pan with the sausage mixture, and toss. Add the Parmesan cheese and serve hot. (You may interchange any of your favorite pasta shapes with the penne.)

SERVES 6

~ *Costolette di Vitello Ripiene* ~
Stuffed Veal Chops

6 large dried porcini mushrooms
6 large 1 inch thick veal chops
12 thin slices fontina cheese
12 thin slices prosciutto or ham
1 cup flour
3 eggs
½ teaspoon salt
½ teaspoon freshly ground black
  pepper
1 cup bread crumbs
6 tablespoons (¾ stick) unsalted
  butter

2 tablespoons olive oil
2 cups sliced fresh mushroom caps
  (save stems and chop for the
  sauce)
3 tablespoons finely chopped
  shallots
3 tablespoons finely chopped onion
3 tablespoons chopped fresh
  rosemary
1 cup dry vermouth
1 cup chicken broth
½ cup porcini liquid

Soak the dried mushrooms in warm water for 15 minutes. Strain the liquid through a fine sieve and reserve the liquid. Rinse the mushrooms, drain thoroughly, and chop.

Cut a pocket in each chop. Place a slice of cheese, a slice of prosciutto, and some of the chopped porcini mushrooms in each pocket. Close the pockets with toothpicks. Place the flour on a piece of waxed paper or aluminum foil. Beat the eggs with the salt and pepper in a shallow dish. Place the bread crumbs on another piece of waxed paper or aluminum foil. Dredge the chops in flour on both sides, then in the beaten eggs, and then in the bread crumbs, pressing the meat into the crumbs so they will adhere.

Heat the butter and oil in a large skillet over medium heat and sauté the fresh sliced mushrooms. Remove them when cooked and set them aside. Then add the chops to the skillet and brown them on both sides over medium heat. After they are browned, place the chops in a large shallow ovenproof dish and bake them in a preheated 350° oven for 10 minutes.

Sauté the shallots, rosemary, onion, and the chopped mushroom stems in the butter remaining in the skillet until golden. Add the vermouth, bring it to a boil, and cook until it is reduced by half. Then add the chicken broth and the ½ cup of reserved porcini liquid. Bring to a boil and cook until the sauce has reduced and slightly thickened.

Arrange the chops on each individual plate, spoon sautéed mushrooms over them, then pour some sauce over the mushrooms.

SERVES 6

~ *Pomodori Fritti* ~
Fried Tomatoes

2 large fresh tomatoes, firm but not
   completely ripe
1 cup bread crumbs
1/3 cup freshly grated Parmesan

   cheese
2 eggs
Salt and freshly ground black pepper
1/2 cup olive oil

Wash and dry the tomatoes and cut them into slices about ½ inch thick. Dry the slices with paper towels. Combine the bread crumbs and Parmesan cheese on a piece of aluminum foil.

Beat the eggs with the salt and pepper in a bowl. Dip the tomato slices in the beaten eggs and then coat with the bread crumb mixture. Heat the oil in a large skillet and when the oil is hot, add the tomato slices. Cook over medium-high heat until golden brown on both sides. Remove the tomato slices from the oil with a slotted spoon and drain on paper towels. Serve hot with the veal chops.

SERVES 6

~ *Mousse di Pesca* ~
Peach Mousse

3¼ cups ripe but firm peaches,
   peeled and sliced
Fruit Fresh® (citric acid)
¾ cup sugar

2 tablespoons Amaretto liqueur
6 egg yolks
½ teaspoon almond extract
1½ cups whipping cream

Purée 1 cup of the sliced peaches in a blender. Sprinkle the remaining peaches with some Fruit Fresh to keep them from turning brown and combine them with ¼ cup of the sugar and the Amaretto. Chill until serving time.

Beat egg yolks and remaining sugar with a mixer on high speed until fluffy, 3 to 4 minutes. Add the almond extract and fold in the peach purée. Whip the cream in a separate bowl until stiff and fold it into the peach mixture. Pour into a 9 by 9-inch glass dish and freeze until semihard. Cover with waxed paper and freeze until hard, about 3 hours.

To serve, remove the mousse from the freezer at least ½ hour before serving to let it soften. Scoop some of the mousse into individual serving dishes and spoon sliced peaches with their juice on top.

SERVES 6

L'Festa del Papa
Father's Day Feast

Lasagne al Forno
Baked Lasagne

Filetto di Manzo ai Pepi
Roast Tenderloin of Beef with Peppercorns

Peperoni con Aglio e Capperi
Peppers with Garlic and Capers

Insalata di Fagioli alla Menta
Beans and Mint Salad

Macedonia di Frutta
Fruit Salad

Caffè
Coffee

SERVES 8 to 10

Although there are no parades or great celebrations to mark Father's Day, we tend to celebrate this day in various ways. I asked my husband and the father of our two daughters to suggest a menu I could prepare on his special day.

He wanted a pasta and one of his favorites is lasagne. He is also fond of beef and opted for a roasted tenderloin. A light accompaniment for the meat and a salad with mint were his suggestions. We both agreed on a colorful pepper dish and a mint and bean salad. For dessert, we chose an array of summer fruits combined in a fruit salad for a refreshing ending to this Father's Day Feast.

Preparations

This is an easy meal to prepare, since you will want to spend time with the honoree and the rest of the family. The lasagna can be made days ahead and then placed in the freezer. You can either defrost it at room temperature or for two days in the refrigerator. Another alternative is to make the lasagna the day before Father's Day and then refrigerate it until baking time.

Early in the day, marinate the beef tenderloin with the crushed peppercorns, cover it with aluminum foil, and store it in the refrigerator. One hour before you plan to cook the tenderloin, remove it from the refrigerator to warm up to room temperature. You can make the peppers the day before, or early on Father's Day and then refrigerate them. Depending on the heat of the day, you can either warm the peppers before serving or serve them at room temperature by removing them from the refrigerator an hour before serving.

If you choose to use the dried beans for the salad, you can boil them days ahead, drain them, and place them in the refrigerator. The day before, make the dressing and assemble the salad. This gives the beans a chance to marinate in the dressing.

The Fruit Salad benefits from being assembled early in the day. This gives the flavors of the fruits a chance to blend.

~ *Lasagne al Forno* ~
Baked Lasagne

MEAT SAUCE:

1 ounce dried porcini mushrooms
5 tablespoons olive oil
1 medium onion, chopped
1 celery stalk, chopped
1 carrot, chopped
2 cloves garlic, chopped
⅓ cup chopped fresh parsley, leaves only
1 pound lean ground beef, such as ground round
½ pound mild Italian sausages, casings removed, crumbled
¼ pound ground veal

¼ pound prosciutto or boiled ham, diced
½ cup dry red wine
3 (28 ounce) cans peeled Italian tomatoes with juice, tomatoes chopped
1 cup beef bouillon
Pinch of red pepper flakes
½ teaspoon grated lemon rind
⅛ teaspoon nutmeg
½ teaspoon salt
½ teaspoon freshly ground black pepper

To make the meat sauce, soak the porcini mushrooms in warm water for 20 minutes.

Heat the oil in a deep, heavy saucepan over medium heat. Add the onion, celery, carrot, garlic, and parsley and sauté until the onion is limp and translucent. Add the beef, sausage, and veal and sauté, stirring often, until the meat loses its color.

Drain the mushrooms, rinse them well under cold water, and chop them. Add the mushrooms and diced ham to the saucepan. Then add the wine, increase the heat to medium high, and cook until all the wine has evaporated. Stir in the chopped tomatoes with their juice, the beef bouillon, red pepper flakes, lemon rind, nutmeg, salt, and pepper. Reduce heat to simmer and continue cooking, uncovered, stirring often, for about 2 hours or until the sauce is thick. Remove the pan from the heat and let the sauce cool for about 1 to 1½ hours before using it. This recipe makes about 2 quarts of sauce.

SALSA BESCIAMELLA:
BECHAMEL (WHITE) SAUCE

4 cups milk
6 tablespoons (¾ stick) unsalted butter

½ cup all-purpose flour
¼ teaspoon freshly grated nutmeg
½ teaspoon salt

To make the béchamel sauce, heat the milk in a saucepan until just below the boiling point. Melt the butter over low heat in another saucepan. When the butter starts to foam, add the flour and stir with a wooden spoon until well blended. Slowly add the hot milk to the flour mixture, stirring in the same direction until the sauce has thickened and is smooth. Add the nutmeg and salt and stir gently. Remove from heat and set aside while preparing the lasagne.

½ pound dried wide lasagne
¾ pound mozzarella cheese,
  coarsely grated

¾ cup freshly grated Parmesan
  cheese

Boil the lasagne in salted boiling water for 10 minutes. Remove the noodles with a slotted spoon and place them immediately in cold water. Lay the noodles flat on a towel to dry.

Butter a 13½ by 9-inch lasagna pan and spread the bottom with a small amount of meat sauce. Arrange the lasagne noodles to cover the bottom of the baking dish, slightly overlapping each noodle. Spread the noodles with the meat sauce, then cover them with a layer of the béchamel sauce. Sprinkle with some of the mozzarella and some Parmesan cheese. Continue layering the noodles, the meat sauce, white sauce, and cheeses up to ½ inch of the top of the pan, ending the last layer with the cheeses.

Bake in a preheated 375° oven for 25 to 30 minutes or until the top is slightly golden. Remove the baking dish from the oven and allow the lasagne to cool for about 10 minutes before cutting and serving.

You may prepare this dish a day in advance. Assemble the dish but do not bake it, wrap in plastic wrap, and place in the refrigerator. Bake the lasagne for 40 minutes in a preheated 375° oven. You can also freeze the lasagna. Wrap it in plastic wrap, then in aluminum foil, and freeze. When ready to use, remove from the freezer to the refrigerator for two days to defrost and then bake in the oven.

SERVES 8 to 10

~ *Filetto di Manzo ai Pepi* ~
Roast Tenderloin of Beef with Peppercorns

¾ cup mixed peppercorns (black,
white, green, and rose)
2 cloves garlic, peeled and cut in
half
4½ to 5 pounds beef tenderloin, fat
trimmed

2 tablespoons olive oil
1 teaspoon salt
8 tablespoons (1 stick) unsalted
butter
½ cup cognac

Place the peppercorns in a dishcloth, crush them with a wooden mallet or the side of a chef's knife, and place the crushed peppercorns on a large platter.

Rub the garlic over all sides of the tenderloin, spread the oil all over it with a brush, and season it with the salt. Place the meat on the platter with the crushed peppercorns and roll it in the peppercorns to coat all of the surfaces of the meat.

Place 2 tablespoons of the butter in a roasting pan over high heat and when the butter begins to sizzle, add the tenderloin and sear it on all sides. Then place the tenderloin in a preheated 450° oven to roast for 30 minutes (medium rare, or 130° to 135° on a meat thermometer), turning the meat over once. Cooking time will vary depending on the actual weight and thickness of the meat.

When the tenderloin has reached the desired doneness, remove it from the oven and place it on a platter; cover it with aluminum foil and keep it warm in the oven with the heat off and the door slightly ajar.

Remove any fat from the surface of the juices in the roasting pan, then place the pan over medium heat, add the cognac, and stir with a wooden spoon to loosen any pepper and pieces of meat attached to the bottom of the pan.

Before serving, cut the tenderloin in thick slices. Pour the juice from the tenderloin into the roasting pan, mixing well, and warm the contents of the pan. Add the remaining 6 tablespoons butter to the sauce mixture and whisk until the butter is completely mixed in with the sauce. Arrange the tenderloin slices on a heated platter and serve. Serve the sauce separately and pass it after the meat has been served. If you prefer, you can strain the sauce to remove any leftover peppercorns.

SERVES 8 to 10

~ *Peperoni con Aglio* ~
Peppers with Garlic a

3½ pounds red and yellow peppers	3 table
5 cloves garlic	½ teas
3 tablespoons capers	½ teas
6 tablespoons olive oil	pep
Pinch of red pepper flakes	4 tables_____ chopped parsley

Clean and cut the peppers into thin strips. Chop the garlic. Rinse the capers, drain, and paper dry them.

Heat the olive oil in a large frying pan over high heat. When the oil is very hot, add the pepper strips and the red pepper flakes and stir while the peppers are cooking. When the peppers begin to get brown on the edges, reduce the heat to medium-high and add the chopped garlic and the capers. Continue stirring while adding the vinegar, salt, and pepper. Let the vinegar evaporate for 1 minute. Add the parsley and continue cooking for 1 more minute while stirring. Serve either hot, at room temperature, or cold with meats.

SERVES 8 to 10

~ *Insalata di Fagioli alla Menta* ~
Beans and Mint Salad

2 (15 ounce) cans cannellini beans or 1 pound dried white beans	7 tablespoons olive oil
	2 tablespoons chopped fresh parsley
2 cloves garlic, finely chopped	2 tablespoons chopped fresh mint
1 tablespoon Dijon mustard	leaves
3 tablespoons red wine vinegar	Freshly ground black pepper
½ teaspoon salt	

If using canned beans drain them or cook the dried white beans al dente, drain, and cool them.

Place the chopped garlic in a large serving bowl. Add the mustard and vinegar and season with salt. Whisk together to blend. Then slowly pour the olive oil into the serving bowl, whisking constantly, until the dressing has thickened and has the consistency of mayonnaise. Add the drained beans, the chopped parsley and mint, and season with freshly ground pepper. Toss thoroughly to mix and serve.

SERVES 8 to 10

~ Macedonia di Frutta ~
Fruit Salad

3 peaches, peeled and cut in cubes

3 nectarines, peeled and cut in cubes

4 pint baskets of different berries in season

6 ounces white grapes, stems removed

6 ounces red grapes, stems removed

½ medium cantaloupe, cut in cubes

3 large slices watermelon, seeds removed, cut in cubes

6 tablespoons sugar

Juice of 1 lemon

½ cup Marsala

Mint leaves, for garnish

Place the prepared fruits in a large glass bowl. Sprinkle the sugar over them and add the lemon juice and Marsala. Mix thoroughly and garnish with fresh mint leaves. Cover and refrigerate for at least 3 hours before serving.

SERVES 8 to 10

Special Occasion Menus

Un Pranzo per l'Anniversario
An Anniversary Dinner

Una Serata con Lume di Candele
An Evening with Candlelight

Un Pranzo per la Coppa Americana di Football
Super Bowl Dinner

Un Compleanno Speciale
A Very Special Birthday Dinner

Una Grande Occasione
A Grand Occasion

Una Cena al Caminetto
A Dinner by the Fireside

Una Cena per l'Innamorati
A Dinner for Lovers

Festa di San Valentino
A Valentine Feast

Festa di Mare
Seafood Feast

Il Ricevimento
Cocktail Party

Un Pranzo per l'Anniversario
An Anniversary Dinner

Prosciutto e Melone
Prosciutto with Melon

Risotto con Zafferano
Saffron Risotto

Ossobuchi
Veal Shanks

Asparagi al Burro e Parmigiano
Asparagus with Butter and Parmesan

Mele Fritte
Apple Fritters

Caffè
Coffee

SERVES 6

Surprise one of your favorite couples with this anniversary dinner and invite another couple to share in the festivities. Present the couple with a small surprise gift and if they like to cook, you might want to write out the recipes for this menu and share them.

The anniversary dinner begins with a very simple but traditional Italian appetizer—Prosciutto and Melon. The melon is refreshing, and it is an old Italian adage that prosciutto is an appetite stimulant.

In Italy Saffron Risotto is frequently served with Ossobuchi, or braised veal shanks. The veal shanks have a very piquant tomato-based sauce. The asparagus are a mild and refreshing complement to the meat.

Apple Fritters, which are made with apples soaked in wine, complete this anniversary dinner.

Preparations

Cut the melon ahead of time and assemble the appetizer just before dinner.

Although the risotto cannot be made ahead, you may want to sauté the onions ahead and set them aside. To make your cooking easier, you can also get the right amounts of wine, rice, and broth ready, so that when you are ready to cook the major ingredients are at hand.

The Ossobuchi can be prepared ahead of time to the point of putting it in the oven. Then set the veal aside and cover it until time to put it in the oven. Be sure to schedule 1½ to 2 hours of cooking time for the Ossobuchi.

The asparagus can be cleaned, cut, and washed early in the day and then stored in the refrigerator until it is time to cook it.

Cut, peel, and marinate the apples just before dinner. You can also prepare the batter at that time. Then cook the dessert just before serving. However, if you are planning to serve the fritters cold, you can cook them in the afternoon. They can also be cooked just before dinner and will still be at room temperature at dessert time.

~ *Prosciutto e M* ~
Prosciutto with N

1 large cantaloupe   *1 lem(*
12 thin slices prosciutto

Cut the melon into 12 slices, remove the i
prosciutto around each slice of melon. Place two slices of melon
wrapped in prosciutto on each of six plates. Serve at room temperature with a wedge of lemon for garnish.

SERVES 6

~ *Risotto con Zafferano* ~
Saffron Risotto

4 cups chicken broth
8 tablespoons (1 stick) unsalted
    butter
1 medium yellow onion, chopped
    fine
½ teaspoon white pepper
½ cup dry white wine

2 cups Italian Arborio rice
1 teaspoon salt
¼ teaspoon saffron or 1 sachet
    saffron powder
½ cup freshly grated Parmesan
    cheese

Heat the broth in a medium saucepan.

Melt 6 tablespoons of the butter in a large saucepan, and when
the butter foams add the onion and white pepper. Sauté over medium
heat until the onion is golden and soft. Add the white wine and cook
over medium heat until the wine is reduced by half. Add the rice and
salt and cook, stirring, for 2 minutes or until the rice is coated with
the pan juices.

Add the hot chicken broth and saffron and stir. Bring to a boil,
cover the pan tightly, and cook over low heat for 15 minutes. The
rice should be tender but firm to the bite. Remove from heat and mix
in the remaining 2 tablespoons butter and the Parmesan cheese. Mix
well and place the rice in a warm dish. Serve immediately with additional Parmesan cheese.

SERVES 6

~ Ossobuchi ~
Veal Shanks

4 hind-quarter veal shanks, each
　　cut by the butcher in 3 pieces
1 teaspoon salt
½ teaspoon freshly ground black
　　pepper
½ cup flour
4 tablespoons olive oil
1 medium yellow onion, chopped
　　fine
1 carrot, chopped
2 celery stalks, chopped
3 tablespoons unsalted butter
2 teaspoons chopped garlic

2 teaspoons grated lemon rind
½ teaspoon grated orange rind
1 cup white dry wine
1 cup chicken broth
1 (16 ounce) can whole tomatoes
　　with their juices, tomatoes
　　coarsely chopped
¼ teaspoon marjoram
2 teaspoons chopped fresh parsley
2 teaspoons chopped fresh basil or
　　1½ teaspoons dried crumbled
　　basil
Pinch of red pepper flakes

Season the pieces of veal shanks with salt and pepper and dredge with flour.

Heat the olive oil in a large heavy skillet over medium-high heat and brown the veal pieces on both sides. While the veal is browning, sauté the onion, carrot, and celery in the butter in an ovenproof casserole or baking dish large enough to hold all of the veal shanks in a single layer. When the vegetables are tender, in about 10 minutes, add the garlic and lemon and orange rinds. Remove the casserole from the heat and place the browned veal shanks on top of the vegetables.

Add the white wine to the skillet in which the veal was browned, bring to a boil, scraping any residue from the bottom of the pan, and cook until the wine is reduced by half. Add the broth, tomatoes, marjoram, parsley, basil, and red pepper flakes; then pour the mixture over the veal shanks in the casserole. Bring the casserole to a simmer on top of the stove, cover tightly, and place in a preheated 350° oven. Cook for about 1½ to 2 hours or until the veal is very tender. Turn the shanks about every 15 minutes. If necessary, add more warm broth.

When the veal is done, the sauce should be thick and creamy. Remove shanks to a warm platter and pour the sauce over the meat. Serve immediately.

SERVES 6

~ *Asparagi al Burro e Parmigiano* ~
Asparagus with Butter and Parmesan

1 pound fresh asparagus
½ cup freshly grated Parmesan

8 tablespoons (1 stick) butter

Trim the tough parts off the ends of the asparagus. Remove the leaves below the tips and cut the asparagus so that all of the stalks are the same length.

Steam the asparagus horizontally in a large pan. Cook until done but still quite firm, about 4 to 5 minutes.

Place the asparagus on a large platter with the tips meeting in the center and sprinkle with Parmesan cheese. Melt the butter in a small saucepan until brown. Pour it over the cheese while the butter is very hot, and it will melt the cheese. Serve immediately.

SERVES 6

~ *Mele Fritte* ~
Apple Fritters

4 large firm apples
1 cup orange juice
½ cup Marsala
2¼ cups all-purpose flour, sifted
½ teaspoon baking powder

1 cup milk
4 egg yolks
¼ cup sugar
Oil for frying, 2 inches deep
Powdered sugar, for garnish

Core and peel the apples and cut them into round slices. Marinate cut apples in a bowl with the orange juice and the Marsala for 15 minutes.

Combine the flour and baking powder. Whisk the sugar and egg yolks together in a large bowl until lemon colored. Beat in the flour mixture and then stir in the milk and beat thoroughly. Add the batter to the apples in their marinade. Stir gently to blend the ingredients. Let the mixture rest for 10 minutes.

Place 2 inches of oil in a deep saucepan. Heat the oil and use a slotted spoon to lower a few apple rounds at a time into the hot oil. Turn the fritters and when golden on both sides remove them from the oil with a slotted spoon. Drain on paper towels. Arrange drained fritters on a platter and sprinkle with powdered sugar. Serve hot or cold.

SERVES 6

Una Serata con Lume di Candele
An Evening with Candlelight

Bresaola
Bresaola

Tortellini con Salsa di Pomodoro
Tortellini with Tomato Sauce

Filetto con Arugula
Fillet of Beef with Arugula

Fagiolini Verdi con Prosciutto e Aglio
Green Beans with Prosciutto and Garlic

Funghi Trifolati
Sautéed Mushrooms

Formaggio e Pere
Cheese and Pears

Biscotti con Vin Santo
Cookies with Vin Santo Wine

Caffè
Coffee

SERVES 6

This is a very special dinner, which when served by candlelight becomes a special occasion. I always feel that the warm glow of candlelight enhances the ambience of a dinner party.

Bresaola, or air-dried beef, served with mushrooms, capers, and Parmesan cheese starts this elegant meal. If bresaola is not available, prosciutto may be substituted.

The tortellini, small dumpling-like pasta filled with meat, are served in a light, creamy tomato sauce. The fillet of beef is simply roasted or broiled on the barbecue and then topped with arugula for additional flavor. Prosciutto and garlic are sautéed with green beans and mushrooms to complement the meat.

Since cheese and fruit frequently end an Italian dinner, I have chosen this as a light ending to the meal. After the dessert enjoy a glass of wine and some Biscotti.

Preparations

Early in the afternoon, you can arrange the bresaola on a large platter with all of the other ingredients except the cheese, which will tend to absorb the juices. Cover and refrigerate the platter until ready to serve. As you are arranging the individual appetizer plates, you can add the cheese.

To really get an advance start on this dinner, make the tomato sauce ahead and freeze it. Before cooking the tortellini defrost and heat the sauce.

You can prepare part of the main course in the afternoon. Marinate the fillet of beef early in the afternoon and chop the arugula for this dish. If you desire, you can also clean the green beans, blanch them for 1 minute, cool them, and paper dry them. The beans can then be refrigerated until you are ready to use them. The mushrooms can be cleaned and set aside.

Cut the cheese in pieces and refrigerate. However, do not cut the pears, since they will turn dark. The Biscotti can be made at your leisure. They can be stored in tins and kept as an addition to many desserts.

~ *Bresaola* ~
Bresaola

30 slices bresaola, cut very thin
2 tablespoons finely chopped Italian
    parsley (use plain parsley if
    Italian parsley is not available)
2 tablespoons capers, drained
4 small white mushrooms, thinly
    sliced

½ cup extra virgin olive oil
Juice of 1 lemon
½ cup slivered fresh Parmesan
    cheese
6 lemon wedges, for garnish
6 fresh parsley sprigs, for garnish

Arrange the slices of bresaola on a large platter. Sprinkle the chopped parsley, capers, and mushroom slices over the bresaola. Then pour the olive oil and lemon juice over the meat and vegetables.

Just before dinner, arrange 5 slices of bresaola with some parsley, capers, mushrooms, oil, and cheese on each plate. Decorate with a lemon wedge and a parsley sprig. Serve with slices of French baguette.

SERVES 6

~ Tortellini con Salsa di Pomodoro ~
Tortellini with Tomato Sauce

4 cups Tomato, Basil Sauce (recipe
  below)
4 tablespoons (½ stick) unsalted
  butter
½ cup whipping cream

2 (12 ounce) packages fresh or
  frozen meat tortellini
⅔ cup freshly grated Parmesan
  cheese

Choose a saucepan large enough to accommodate the tortellini later. Place the prepared tomato sauce in it and warm over medium heat. Add the butter and cream and stir thoroughly. Cook for 5 minutes, then turn off the heat.

While the sauce is warming up, boil the tortellini until tender but al dente. (Fresh tortellini cook much faster than dried.) Drain well and transfer to the saucepan with the tomato sauce. Toss to combine the pasta and sauce.

Place the tortellini and sauce in a warm serving bowl or on a warm platter. Add the grated cheese, mix well, and serve at once. If desired, heat some of the leftover sauce and serve it in a gravy boat. Additional grated cheese may also be served.

SALSA DI POMODORO, BASILICO AGLIO:
TOMATO, BASIL SAUCE

½ cup extra virgin olive oil
4 medium cloves garlic, cut in half
2 large (28 ounce) cans peeled
  tomatoes with juice, tomatoes
  chopped coarsely

½ teaspoon salt
½ teaspoon freshly ground pepper
Pinch of red pepper flakes
1 cup fresh basil, chopped

Place the olive oil and garlic in a medium saucepan and cook over medium heat until the garlic is golden brown. Discard the garlic, add the chopped tomatoes with their juice, salt, pepper, and red pepper flakes. Then add the chopped basil and mix thoroughly.

Cook, uncovered, over medium-low heat for 30 minutes to let some of the juice evaporate, stirring occasionally. Makes about 6 cups of sauce.

SERVES 6

~ *Filetto con Arugula* ~
Fillet of Beef with Arugula

3½ pound fillet of beef
1 tablespoon dry Italian seasoning
¼ teaspoon salt
¼ teaspoon freshly ground pepper

2 cloves garlic, chopped
½ cup extra virgin olive oil
1 cup fresh arugula, chopped fine
Freshly ground pepper

Place the fillet of beef on a platter. Sprinkle it with the Italian seasoning, salt, pepper, and garlic on all sides. Add ¼ cup of the olive oil and turn the meat to coat it on all sides. Marinate for several hours or more in the refrigerator. Bring the beef to room temperature before cooking it. Roast the fillet in a preheated 425° oven for 45 minutes for rare meat (125° to 130° on a meat thermometer). The fillet may also be cooked on a barbecue on high heat, turning it every 5 minutes, for 45 minutes.

Let the meat stand for 10 minutes before carving. Slice the meat into ½ inch thick slices and arrange them on a heated platter. Sprinkle the chopped arugula over the meat. Add the remaining olive oil, the juice from the meat, and some freshly ground black pepper. Serve immediately.

SERVES 6

~ *Fagiolini Verdi con Prosciutto e Aglio* ~
Green Beans with Prosciutto and Garlic

1½ pounds fresh green beans
⅓ cup extra virgin olive oil
1 thick slice prosciutto, cut in thin
  strips

3 cloves garlic, chopped
¼ teaspoon salt
¼ teaspoon freshly ground black
  pepper

Snap the ends off the beans and rinse them in cold water. Bring a large pot of water to a boil and add the green beans. Bring to a boil again and boil for only 1 minute.

Drain the beans immediately and stop the cooking process by putting them in cold water and adding ice cubes. When the beans are cold, drain them and pat them dry with paper towels. Set the beans aside.

Choose a skillet large enough to accommodate all of the green beans. Add the oil and over medium heat sauté the prosciutto strips for a few minutes. Then add the beans and chopped garlic. Sprinkle with the salt and pepper and mix thoroughly. Cook on medium-high heat, stirring often to prevent burning, for 10 to 15 minutes, depending on the thickness of the beans. Place the beans on a heated platter and serve immediately.

SERVES 6

~ *Funghi Trifolati* ~
Sautéed Mushrooms

1½ pounds small white mushrooms
2 tablespoons butter
2 tablespoons extra virgin olive oil
¼ cup parsley, chopped

3 cloves garlic, chopped
¼ teaspoon salt
¼ teaspoon freshly ground black
  pepper

Wash and dry the mushrooms thoroughly and cut them in half. Melt the butter with the oil in a large skillet. When the butter foams, add the mushrooms. Sauté over medium-high heat until golden; add the parsley, garlic, salt, and pepper. Cook 1 minute longer. Do not over-cook the parsley or garlic. Place the mushrooms in a heated bowl and serve hot.

SERVES 6

~ *Formaggio e Pere* ~
Cheese and Pears

4 firm pears
1 basket raspberries or any other

berries in season
1 pound fontina cheese

Wash and dry the pears. Slice them in half lengthwise, and remove the cores and stems. Cut each half in three equal parts. Clean the berries and cut the cheese in wide strips.

To serve, arrange 4 slices of pear and 2 strips of cheese in the shape of a fan on each of 6 individual dessert plates. Place 3 berries under each fan.

SERVES 6

~ *Biscotti con Vin Santo* ~
Cookies with Wine

Vin Santo is a sweet Italian dessert wine kept for special occasions. It is served after dinner with Biscotti. If the Vin Santo is not available, you may substitute sweet vermouth, Marsala, or port wine.

The Biscotti are dry, crunchy, hard cookies because they are baked twice. They will soften up immediately when dipped in wine. They are also tasty when dipped in coffee. Kept in a cookie tin, the Biscotti will last for months.

Serve the Vin Santo in a brandy snifter placed on a small plate and serve with a side dish of the biscotti.

BISCOTTI:

3 cups all-purpose flour
1½ teaspoons baking powder
¼ teaspoon salt
4 eggs
1 cup sugar
1 teaspoon vanilla extract
1 teaspoon almond extract

3 tablespoons Amaretto liqueur or brandy
8 tablespoons (1 stick) unsalted butter, melted
1 cup walnuts, almonds, or hazelnuts, coarsely chopped

Pour the flour in a mound on a work surface or in a big bowl. Make a well in the center and in the well place the baking powder and salt.

Beat 3 of the eggs in a medium bowl and add the sugar, vanilla and almond extracts, Amaretto or brandy, and the melted butter. Add this mixture to the center of the well. Gradually work the flour into the ingredients in the well and mix with your hands or a wooden spoon until smooth. Knead in the nuts thoroughly and keep kneading, sprinkling additional flour if necessary. Place the bowl in the refrigerator for about 15 minutes.

Butter and flour two baking sheets. Divide the dough in quarters. Roll each piece of dough on a floured surface into a 2 to 3 inch wide log and place the logs at least 3 inches apart on the baking sheets.

Beat the remaining egg and brush it over the tops of the dough logs. Bake in a preheated 350° oven for 20 minutes. Remove the logs from the oven and reduce the heat to 325°. Cut the logs diagonally into 1-inch slices and lay them cut side up on the baking sheets. Return to the oven for another 15 minutes. Cool on racks. Store the Biscotti in a cookie tin.

6 DOZEN COOKIES

Un Pranzo per la Coppa Americana di Football
Super Bowl Dinner

Antipasti con Peperoni Arrostiti
Appetizers with Roasted Peppers

Pollo Fritto
Fried Chicken

Carciofi Rosolati
Sautéed Artichokes

Patate con Pancetta e Erbe
Potatoes with Pancetta and Herbs

Mousse degli Angeli
Angels' Mousse

Caffè
Coffee

SERVES 8

The climax of the entire professional football season in the United States is the Super Bowl. Watching the game on television has become a ritual in many American homes. The Italians, too, are very interested in who will win the Super Bowl title.

Since the event is one of American origin I have opted to use the American favorite, Fried Chicken, which is also a dish of upper Tuscany, for the entrée. Assorted cold cuts with roasted peppers begin this dinner. Fried Chicken is accompanied by sautéed artichokes and potatoes. A light mousse completes this Super Bowl Dinner.

Preparations

The mixed cold cuts can be purchased at the delicatessen and assembled the morning of the game, then refrigerated. (If you do not have access to an Italian delicatessen, substitute other cold cuts for the ones specified in the menu.) You can prepare the peppers anytime during the week.

So that you can enjoy the game, brown the chicken on both sides in the morning, place it in a roasting pan, and set aside until about 20 minutes before the game ends. Then put the chicken in a preheated 350° oven and bake for 20 minutes and keep the chicken warm.

The artichokes can be prepared the day before, cooked, and then stored in the refrigerator. The next day they can be warmed up and served either hot or at room temperature.

You can prepare the vegetables and pancetta for the potatoes early in the day, as well as cooking the potatoes. Then you just have to warm and assemble the dish before serving dinner.

Depending on your preference, the dessert can be made a day ahead or early in the morning before the game.

~ *Antipasti con Peperoni Arrostiti* ~
Appetizers with Roasted Peppers

8 thin slices prosciutto
8 thin slices coppa
8 thin slices mortadella
8 thin slices sopressata
8 thin slices salami

8 thin slices boiled ham
Green onions, black olives,
*   radishes, and canned artichoke*
*   hearts, for garnish*
Roasted peppers (recipe follows)

On a large platter, arrange the cold cuts and garnish with some green onions, black olives, radishes, and artichoke hearts. Serve this antipasto with roasted peppers and slices of French bread.

PEPERONI ARROSTITI:
ROASTED PEPPERS

3 red peppers
2 yellow peppers
5 tablespoons extra virgin olive oil
¼ teaspoon vinegar
¼ teaspoon sugar
2 tablespoons chopped parsley

2 cloves garlic, chopped fine
1 teaspoon capers, chopped
¼ teaspoon salt
¼ teaspoon freshly ground black
*   pepper*

Cut the peppers in half and remove the seeds. Wash the peppers and dry them with paper towels. Place them, cut side down, on a baking sheet and roast under the broiler until the skin begins to blister and is dark brown. (The peppers may also be roasted over an open flame of a gas cooktop.) Remove the peppers from the oven and place them in a brown paper bag. Close the bag and set aside for 10 minutes. Remove the peppers from the bag and peel the skin. Then cut the peppers into 1 inch wide strips. Arrange them on a medium platter so that they overlap.

Combine the oil, vinegar, sugar, parsley, garlic, capers, salt, and pepper in a small bowl. Pour the dressing over the peppers and marinate. Refrigerate for several hours or overnight. Serve at room temperature.

SERVES 8

~ *Pollo Fritto* ~
Fried Chicken

*8 chicken breasts halves, boneless
and skinless
8 chicken thighs, skinless
1 teaspoon salt
1 teaspoon freshly ground black
pepper*

*½ teaspoon granulated garlic
1 cup all-purpose flour
4 eggs, beaten
1 cup olive oil
1 lemon, cut in wedges*

Wash and dry the chicken pieces, place them on a platter, and season with ½ teaspoon each of the salt and pepper, and the garlic. Spread the flour on a piece of aluminum foil. Beat the eggs in a bowl with the remaining ½ teaspoons of salt and pepper.

Heat the olive oil in a large frying pan or cast iron skillet over high heat. While the oil is getting hot, dredge the chicken pieces in flour on both sides, then dip the pieces in the egg mixture, letting the excess egg drip off. Place the chicken pieces in the hot oil and fry for 12 to 15 minutes on each side or until golden brown and cooked through. Drain on paper towels and place the chicken pieces on a warm platter. Garnish with lemon wedges and serve.

To partially cook the chicken ahead, fry it only for 6 minutes on each side. Then remove the chicken pieces from the skillet and placed them in a roasting pan, cover with foil, and set aside. A half hour before the dinner put the chicken pan, uncovered, in a preheated 350° oven and cook for 20 more minutes.

SERVES 8

ırciofi Rosolati ~
ıtéed Artichokes

; large	1 teaspoon salt
	1 cup dry white wine
	4 medium cloves garlic, chopped
....virgin olive oil	fine
4 tablespoons (½ stick) butter	4 tablespoons chopped fresh parsley
1 teaspoon freshly ground black	1 cup chicken broth
pepper	

Remove the stems of the artichokes and remove the hard outer leaves with your fingers until only the pale leaves with green at the tips remain at the base of the artichoke. Cut off about 1 inch from the top, making sure you have eliminated all the dark green parts of the leaves. Rub the cut edges with the lemon half.

Cut the trimmed artichokes into quarters. Using a paring knife scrape away the inner choke and curly prickly leaves. Slice the quarters again in half and sprinkle with a little lemon juice. If you are using the small artichokes, do the same thing as above except cut the artichokes only in quarters. Place them in a bowl with cold water and the remainder of the lemon juice for 10 minutes. Drain the artichokes and pat them thoroughly dry with a paper towel.

Place the olive oil and butter in a large sauté pan over medium heat. When the butter starts to foam, add the artichokes and sprinkle with the salt and pepper. Stir and turn the artichokes three or four times. Cook them for 10 minutes. Then add the wine and let evaporate for 1 minute. Add the garlic, parsley, and broth and mix thoroughly. Cover the pan and reduce the heat to low. Cook until the artichokes are tender when pricked with a fork, about 20 minutes, depending on the freshness of the vegetables. If there is too much liquid in the pan when they are done, uncover the pan and increase the heat to evaporate the extra liquid. Serve the artichokes hot or at room temperature.

SERVES 8

~ *Patate con Pancetta e Erbe* ~
Potatoes with Pancetta and Herbs

12 medium red potatoes, unpeeled
½ cup extra virgin olive oil
1 cup small strips pancetta or bacon
2 cups coarsely chopped celery
6 scallions, chopped coarsely including half of the green stems

4 tablespoons chopped fresh parsley
3 tablespoons chopped garlic
½ teaspoon salt
½ teaspoon freshly ground black pepper
Pinch of red pepper flakes

Wash and rinse the potatoes and cut them into quarters. Place them in a large pot and boil them, unpeeled, in plenty of water. Cook the potatoes until just tender when pricked with a fork, about 15 to 20 minutes. When done, drain them.

Heat the oil over medium heat in a large sauté pan that will later be able to accommodate all the potatoes. Add the pancetta, celery, scallions, parsley, and garlic and sauté for about 7 minutes, or until the onions are limp. Add the drained potatoes, and season with salt and pepper and the red pepper flakes. Stir to combine and cook for another 5 minutes. Serve hot. SERVES 8

~ *Mousse degli Angeli* ~
Angels' Mousse

5 eggs, separated
¾ cup sugar
6 tablespoons Frangelico liqueur
1½ envelopes unflavored gelatin
⅓ cup cold water

1½ cups whipping cream
1½ teaspoons vanilla extract
½ cup finely chopped toasted hazelnuts

Beat the egg yolks until light and lemon colored. Add the sugar gradually and continue beating until creamy. Then add the Frangelico liqueur.

Soften the gelatin in ⅓ cup of cold water in a small saucepan; stir over low heat until dissolved. Stir gelatin into the yolk mixture.

Beat the egg whites until stiff but not dry and fold them into the egg yolks. Whip the cream until stiff, add the vanilla, and gently fold into the mousse. Finally fold in the hazelnuts. Pour the mousse into 8 cocktail or sherbet glasses. Chill for at least 2 hours before serving. SERVES 8

Un Compleanno Speciale
A Very Special Birthday Dinner

Bresaola con Carciofi
Bresaola with Artichokes

Zuppa ai Frutti di Mare con Bruschetta
Seafood Soup with Toasted Garlic Bread

Insalata Verde
Green Salad

Crema di Zabaglione Fredda
Chilled Zabaglione Cream

Caffè
Coffee

SERVES 8

Birthdays are special, and there is no better way to celebrate a birthday than to prepare the honoree's favorite foods. It can be an elegant affair or a casual party, depending on the type of food and the atmosphere you wish to create.

The dishes on this menu are the ones I recently prepared for my daughter's birthday. She likes any kind of fish, especially crab, and I thought it would be perfect to celebrate the occasion with a seafood soup. This soup of Italian origin is also known as "Cioppino" in the San Francisco area. Traditionally this soup was made in Italy, as well as in California, with the catch of the day. Whatever kind of seafood the fisherman brought home became the basis of this stew-like dish.

The seafood soup is made with a variety of shellfish and some fin fish. The more variety there is, the better the flavor. If Dungeness crabs are unavailable in your area, substitute another type of crab or add crabmeat at the end of the cooking period.

To start the birthday dinner, I served bresaola with artichokes, which is an appetizer that blends well with fish soup. (If bresaola is not available, prosciutto may be substituted.) The seafood soup was served with toasted garlic bread. A very simple, delicate salad and dressing was a refreshing palate cleanser after the seafood. A chilled zabaglione cream topped with shaved chocolate completed the birthday dinner.

Preparations

Many of the preparations for this birthday dinner can be done before the party. You can prepare the Bresaola with Artichokes early in the afternoon and place it in the refrigerator.

Make the sauce for the soup early in the day or even the day before. However, you will want to add the seafood just before dinner to prevent overcooking.

Early in the day you can wash and prepare the salad greens and store them in the refrigerator. Since the dressing takes only a few minutes to make, you will probably opt to do that just before serving the salad.

The dessert can be made the day before and chilled. At the same time you can shave the chocolate and have it ready when serving the dessert.

~ *Bresaola con Carciofi* ~
Bresaola with Artichokes

24 paper-thin slices bresaola or
    prosciutto
1 (8½ ounce) can artichoke hearts,
    sliced
2 tablespoons chopped fresh parsley
⅓ cup chopped fresh arugula

Juice of 1 lemon
⅓ cup extra virgin olive oil
1 tablespoon capers, drained
¼ cup slivered fresh Parmesan
    cheese
8 sprigs parsley, for garnish

Arrange the slices of bresaola on a large platter. Try not to overlap the slices too much. Place the artichoke slices over the meat. Sprinkle with parsley and arugula. Squeeze the lemon juice over the top, then pour the olive oil over the top, and add the capers and slivers of cheese. Cover with parchment or waxed paper and refrigerate until ready to serve.

Arrange three slices of bresaola (or prosciutto) with some slices of artichokes, and pieces of parsley, arugula, capers, cheese, and some of the oil on each of 8 plates. Decorate with a sprig of parsley and serve with slices of French bread.

SERVES 8

~ *Zuppa ai Frutti di Mare con Bruschetta* ~
Seafood Soup with Toasted Garlic Bread

¾ cup extra virgin olive oil
1 medium onion, finely chopped
4 scallions, white parts only,
    chopped
1 celery stalk, finely chopped
1 medium carrot, finely chopped
4 cloves garlic, chopped
½ cup chopped parsley
1 small hot red chili pepper, minced
1⅓ cups dry white wine
2 (28 ounce) cans Italian peeled
    tomatoes with their juice,
    tomatoes finely chopped
1 (28 ounce) can tomato purée

½ teaspoon dried oregano
½ teaspoon salt
¼ teaspoon freshly ground pepper
3 raw Dungeness crabs, cracked
    and cleaned
1¾ pounds fresh clams
1¼ pounds fresh mussels
1¾ pounds medium fresh shrimp
2 tablespoons unsalted butter
2 pounds firm-fleshed fish, cubed
16 ½-inch slices of firm, coarse-
    textured French bread
4 large cloves garlic, peeled and cut
    in half

Select a saucepan large enough to accommodate all of the seafood. Heat the oil in this saucepan over medium heat. Add the onion, scallions, celery, carrot, garlic, parsley, and chili pepper and cook until the onion begins to color. Add the white wine and let it evaporate for a few minutes.

Add the chopped tomatoes with their juice, the tomato purée with 1 cup of water, the oregano, salt, and pepper and mix thoroughly. Bring to a boil and cook, covered, on low heat for 20 minutes.

Soak the clams for ½ hour in cold water, scrub them with a brush, and rinse again. Clean and rinse the mussels. Shell and devein the shrimp and rinse them in cold water.

Melt the butter in a small skillet over medium high heat and sauté the fish for a few minutes until it is opaque. Bring the soup to a boil and add the cleaned crabs, mussels, clams, shrimp, and sautéed fish. Mix thoroughly and cook for 5 to 7 minutes over medium heat or until the clams and mussels open, stirring often to mix the flavors.

Bake the slices of bread in the oven until golden. Remove from the oven and rub each slice with garlic. Place a slice of bread in the bottom of each soup dish, cover with fish soup, and serve very hot. Serve the remaining bread slices separately.

Any leftover fish soup can be warmed and tossed with spaghetti to make a meal for the following evening.

SERVES 8

~ *Insalata Verde* ~
Green Salad

1 head butter lettuce
1 head red lettuce
1 small head red radicchio
1/3 cup watercress
1/3 cup coarsely chopped arugula
1/3 cup Italian parsley leaves

Salt and freshly ground pepper, to
taste
1/3 cup extra virgin olive oil
2 tablespoons red wine vinegar
Freshly ground pepper

Trim, wash, and dry the salad greens and tear them into bite-sized pieces. Remove the stems from the watercress and the parsley. Place all the greens in a large salad bowl. Dissolve the salt in the vinegar and sprinkle over the salad. Pour the oil over the salad and mix well. Add freshly ground pepper and mix again. Serve at once.

SERVES 8

~ *Crema di Zabaglione Fredda* ~
Chilled Zabaglione Cream

6 tablespoons sugar
1/2 cup Marsala
6 egg yolks
1 tablespoon brandy
1 tablespoon vanilla extract
3 egg whites

1/8 teaspoon salt
1/8 teaspoon cream of tartar
1 cup whipping cream
1 square (1 ounce) semisweet
chocolate

Mix together 4 tablespoons of the sugar and the Marsala in the top of a double boiler. Beat the egg yolks until light and lemon colored and add them to the Marsala mixture. Cook over hot water, stirring constantly, until thickened. Remove from heat and stir in the brandy and vanilla. Cool.

Beat the egg whites until foamy, add the salt and cream of tartar, and beat until stiff. Then beat in the remaining 2 tablespoons sugar. Fold into the cooled egg yolk mixture. Whip the cream until stiff and fold it into the custard. Spoon into tall, slender parfait glasses or dessert dishes. Chill for 1 hour or longer. Use a vegetable peeler to make chocolate curls from the square of chocolate. Garnish the custard with chocolate curls.

SERVES 8

Una Grande Occasione
A Grand Occasion

Filetti di Salmone
Salmon Fillets

Fettuccine con Crema e Formaggio
Fettuccine in Cream and Cheese Sauce

Filetto con Brandy
Filet Mignons with Brandy

Funghi Saltati al Prezzemolo
Sautéed Mushrooms with Parsley

Insalata di Lattuga con Gorgonzola
Romaine Lettuce with Gorgonzola

Spuma di Cioccolata
Chocolate Mousse

Caffè
Coffee

SERVES 6

A grand occasion can celebrate a raise for the spouse, news of becoming grandparents, or starting on a new career. It is a reason for a
celebration with friends and to enjoy a meal together. You may want
to add some special touches such as your best china and flowers for
the dining room table.

This five-course meal begins with a smoked salmon appetizer,
which has been enhanced with an oil dressing and is served with
slices of French bread. The Fettuccine in Cream and Cheese Sauce is
a light second course, tempting guests to have seconds. However,
there are three more courses to follow.

The Filet Mignon with Brandy is an elegant entrée that is simple to prepare. It is accompanied by Sautéed Mushrooms, which have been a perfect companion to beef for a long time.

The salad with Gorgonzola is a tangy interlude between the beef and the rich Chocolate Mousse, which ends this Grand Occasion.

Preparations

Several items on this menu can be prepared ahead. You can make the salmon appetizer several hours in advance and place it in the refrigerator until serving time.

Since the fettuccine does not take long to prepare and the sauce is best served fresh, you should make the second course just before sitting down to dinner. The sauce does not take long and can be made while the pasta is cooking.

About 10 minutes before dinner, you should cook the filet mignons and finish them up to the point of putting them back in the sauce, which should be done just before serving. If you have time, the mushrooms can be made earlier and the cooking process stopped before they are completely cooked. They can be finished just before dinner.

Several hours before the guests arrive, you can clean the lettuce, spin dry it, break it into bite-sized pieces, and place it in the refrigerator. Also toast the walnuts and crumble the cheese for the salad and set them aside until serving time.

Make the dessert the day before or early in the morning of the party.

~ *Filetti di Salmone* ~
Salmon Fillets

12 large slices smoked salmon
4 teaspoons finely chopped onion
4 teaspoons finely chopped fresh
    parsley

1 tablespoon capers, drained
3 tablespoons extra virgin olive oil
Juice of 1 lemon
6 sprigs fresh parsley, for garnish

Arrange the slices of smoked salmon on a large platter. Sprinkle them with the chopped onion, parsley, and capers. Drizzle the olive oil and lemon juice over the salmon slices and refrigerate.

To serve, arrange two slices of salmon with the sauce and capers on each of 6 plates. Garnish with a sprig of fresh parsley and serve with slices of French bread.

SERVES 6

~ *Fettuccine con Crema e Formaggio* ~
Fettuccine in Cream and Cheese Sauce

1 pound fresh or dried fettuccine
½ cup (8 tablespoons) unsalted
    butter
1 cup whipping cream
¼ teaspoon nutmeg

Salt and white pepper, to taste
1 cup freshly grated Parmesan
    cheese
Additional Parmesan cheese

Cook the fettuccine, uncovered, in boiling salted water until tender but firm to the bite.

While the pasta is cooking, melt the butter in a large skillet. When the butter foams, add the cream and nutmeg. Cook the mixture over medium heat for 2 to 4 minutes until it is slightly thickened. Season with the salt and pepper.

Drain the fettuccine and place it in the pan with the cream sauce. Add the Parmesan cheese. Toss the pasta and sauce until well mixed. Serve immediately with additional Parmesan cheese.

SERVES 6

~ *Filetto con Brandy* ~
Filet Mignons with Brandy

6 filet mignons, 1 inch thick
Salt and pepper, to taste
2 tablespoons tomato sauce
3 tablespoons Dijon mustard
4 drops Worcestershire sauce
1/8 teaspoon cayenne pepper

2 tablespoons butter
3 tablespoons olive oil
1/3 cup brandy
1/2 cup whipping cream
1/4 teaspoon salt

Lightly season the filet mignons with salt and pepper. Combine the tomato sauce, mustard, Worcestershire sauce, and cayenne pepper in a small bowl.

Melt the butter with the oil in a large skillet. When the butter foams, add the meat and cook over medium-high heat for a few minutes on each side or until lightly seared. Remove the meat from the skillet and add the brandy; deglaze the pan. Add the mustard mixture, cream, and salt and mix to blend. Return the meat to the skillet and cook over medium heat to the desired doneness. Place the meat on a warm platter and spoon the sauce over it.

SERVES 6

~ *Funghi Saltati al Prezzemolo* ~
Sautéed Mushrooms with Parsley

1 1/2 pounds medium white
    mushrooms
4 tablespoons olive oil
1/2 small onion, chopped
2 large cloves garlic, peeled and cut
    in half

1/4 cup dry white wine
1/4 teaspoon salt
1/4 teaspoon freshly ground black
    pepper
2 tablespoons chopped fresh parsley
1 tablespoon grated Parmesan cheese

Wash and dry the mushrooms and cut them into thick slices.

Heat the oil in a large skillet, add the onion and garlic, and sauté over medium-high heat until the garlic is golden. Add the sliced mushrooms and sauté for 7 to 10 minutes or until the mushrooms are golden and the juice has evaporated. Add the wine and let it evaporate. Season with the salt and pepper. Discard the garlic, add the chopped parsley, and sprinkle the Parmesan cheese over the top.

SERVES 6

~ *Insalata di Lattuga con Gorgonzola* ~
Romaine Lettuce with Gorgonzola

1 head Romaine lettuce
6 tablespoons extra virgin olive oil
1 tablespoon wine vinegar
½ teaspoon salt
1 teaspoon freshly ground pepper

½ cup walnuts, toasted and
  coarsely chopped
¼ pound Gorgonzola cheese,
  crumbled

Wash the lettuce, spin dry, and tear into bite-sized pieces.

Whisk the olive oil, vinegar, salt, and pepper together in a salad bowl. Add the lettuce and toss it thoroughly. Taste and correct the seasoning, if necessary.

Divide the salad among 6 plates, sprinkle with the chopped walnuts, and place the Gorgonzola in the center of the lettuce. Serve immediately.

SERVES 6

~ *Spuma di Cioccolata* ~
Chocolate Mousse

8 ounces semisweet chocolate
3 eggs
1 cup whipping cream
Whipped cream, for garnish

Grated chocolate, for garnish
½ cup sliced almonds, for garnish
  (optional)

Melt the chocolate in the top of a double boiler over hot water. Cool slightly.

Beat the eggs until foamy in a medium bowl. Add the eggs slowly, a little at a time, to the cooled chocolate, beating at low speed. Whip the whipping cream in a large bowl until stiff. Fold the chocolate mixture into the whipped cream.

Spoon the mousse into individual glasses. Refrigerate overnight. Before serving, decorate with additional whipped cream and grated chocolate. Top with sliced almonds, if desired.

SERVES 6

Una Cena al Caminetto
A Dinner by the Fireside

Risotto con Carciofi
Risotto with Artichokes

Pollastrelli con Erbe
Young Chickens with Herbs

Patatine Arrostite al Rosmarino
Small Roasted Potatoes with Rosemary

Indivia Saporita
Tasty Endive

Dolce di Limone Freddo
Frozen Lemon Soufflé

Caffè
Coffee

SERVES 4

In Italy where I grew up, we ate all of the meals in the kitchen in the winter and in the summer. In the winter we always had a fire in the fireplace and for me that was always a very special time. It was cozy and romantic.

To recreate this homey and romantic feeling, my husband and I often invite another couple to share dinner by the fireside. It is so pleasant and beautiful to see the flames reflected on our friends' faces—flames that create dancing shadows on the walls.

In order to enjoy the warmth of the fire with our guests, I chose a menu with items that could be prepared ahead. The dinner starts with Risotto with Artichokes. The entrée consists of broiled chickens, which have been flavored with herbs and are accompanied by roasted potatoes. A tasty endive salad is prepared with a warm dressing. A light lemon dessert concludes this dinner by the fireside.

Preparations

The dessert should be made the day before the p

You can prepare the sauce for the risotto early in
sauce aside, add the rice before dinner, and finish cook
at that time.

The chicken benefits from marinating in the herbs and o
your schedule permits, early in the afternoon you can prepa
chickens, chop the herbs, and combine them with the olive oil in
pan in which you will later broil the chickens. However, if marina
ing the chickens early in the afternoon, place them in the refrigerator
and turn them every 30 minutes.

In the afternoon you can also clean the potatoes and put them in
the pan with all of the ingredients except the wine. You may also
sauté the ham, pancetta, onion, and mushrooms for the salad and set
this aside until later. The endive can be cleaned, covered with paper
towels, and refrigerated.

The last-minute dinner preparations can be done before you
serve the first course, since the dishes will stay warm and the salad is
also served warm. Forty minutes before dinner, place the chicken in
the oven under the broiler and put the potatoes in another oven. (If
you have only one oven, prepare the potatoes ahead of time and reheat just before dinner.) Fifteen minutes before dinner, you will
want to finish cooking the rice. About 10 minutes before dinner, heat
the salad ingredients, add the endive, and finish cooking the warm
salad.

Before sitting down to dinner, remove the dessert from the freezer
and place it in the refrigerator to soften while you and your guests
enjoy the meal.

arciofi ~
chokes

lespoons chopped fresh parsley
spoon salt
spoon freshly ground pepper
ips beef broth, or 1 (14½
ince) can beef broth diluted
ith 1½ cups water
ups Italian Arborio rice
lespoons freshly grated
    Parmesan cheese

Discard the outer leaves of the artichokes and cut off the hard tips. Cut the trimmed artichokes into quarters. With a paring knife scrape away the inner choke and the small, curled prickly leaves. Slice the quarters lengthwise as thinly as possible. Place the sliced artichokes in a bowl of cold water with the lemon juice for 10 minutes. Drain and pat dry with paper towels.

Melt 2 tablespoons of the butter and the oil in a medium saucepan over medium heat. Sauté the onions until translucent; add the prosciutto and sauté for a few more minutes. Add the sliced artichokes, garlic, 2 tablespoons of the parsley, the salt and pepper, and ½ cup of the beef broth. Stir and simmer uncovered for about 10 minutes or until the liquid has almost evaporated.

Add the rice and increase the heat to medium-high. Stir the rice thoroughly several times to coat the grains with the pan juices. Add the remaining broth and bring to a boil. Reduce the heat to low and simmer, covered, for 15 minutes or until the rice is done. It should be firm but tender. Remove the saucepan from the heat, add the remaining 2 tablespoons butter, the grated cheese, and the remaining 2 tablespoons parsley. Stir thoroughly and serve at once.

SERVES 4

~ *Pollastrelli con Erbe*
Young Chickens with Herbs

2 young small chickens, about 2 to
2½ pounds each
1 teaspoon salt
1 teaspoon freshly ground black
pepper
2 tablespoons extra virgin olive oil
1 tablespoon chopped fresh
rosemary

1 tablespoon chopped fresh
leaves
1 teaspoon chopped fresh thyme
1 teaspoon chopped fresh marjoram
1 teaspoon chopped fresh oregano
1 teaspoon dry Italian seasoning
4 cloves garlic, peeled and cut in
half

NOTE: If fresh herbs are not available, substitute 2 tablespoons dried Italian herbs for the assorted fresh herbs called for in the list of ingredients and eliminate the additional 1 teaspoon Italian seasoning also called for.

Split the chickens and place each half breast side down on a cutting board and pound as flat as possible with a mallet. Wash the chickens in cold water and pat dry with paper towels.

Season the chickens with the salt and pepper on both sides. Choose a broiler or ovenproof pan that can accommodate all of the chicken pieces in one layer. Coat the bottom of the pan with 2 tablespoons of oil and place the chicken halves on it, skin side up. Sprinkle the chopped herbs (or dried herbs) over the chickens and place the garlic halves on top. Marinate for 30 minutes at room temperature, turning every 10 minutes, ending the cycle with the chickens skin side up.

Preheat the broiler to 400°. Place the chicken on the top shelf of the oven and broil for 30 to 35 minutes or until done, depending on the size of the chickens. While broiling, turn them every 5 minutes. The chickens should be golden. Discard the garlic.

Place the chicken halves on a heated platter and pour the cooking juices and herbs over the top. Decorate the platter with branches of fresh rosemary and bunches of fresh sage, if available. Serve a half chicken per person.

NOTE: The chicken may be marinated up to 1 hour at room temperature or longer in the refrigerator. The longer it marinates, the more intense herb flavor it will have. If marinated in the refrigerator, bring the chickens to room temperature before broiling.

SERVES 4

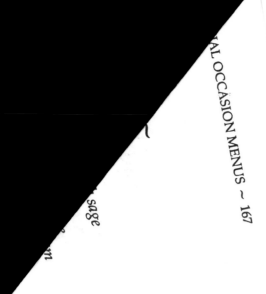

...e al Rosmarino ~
...s with Rosemary

...easpoon salt
...easpoon freshly ground black
...pepper
...inches fresh rosemary, leaves
...nly
...dry white wine

...cold water with a brush and pat them dry with
...owels. Do not remove the skins.

Melt the butter and the oil in a baking dish large enough to accommodate the potatoes in one layer. Add the potatoes and garlic and sauté on medium-high heat for a few minutes. Season with the salt and pepper and add the rosemary leaves; mix well. Sprinkle the wine over the potatoes.

Place the potatoes in a preheated 375° oven for 30 to 40 minutes or until done, depending on the size of the potatoes. While cooking, turn the potatoes after 20 minutes and brush them with the pan juices. Remove the potatoes from the oven when the skin is crispy and the potatoes are tender. Serve at once with the chicken.

SERVES 4

~ Indivia Saporita ~
Tasty Endive

3 large or 4 small Belgian endives
1 slice ham (about 2 ounces), cut in
    cubes
2 thick slices pancetta or bacon, cut
    in small cubes
4 tablespoons extra virgin olive oil
½ onion, chopped
½ pound mushrooms, sliced thin
¼ teaspoon salt
¼ teaspoon freshly ground black
    pepper
3 tablespoons chopped fresh parsley

Wash and drain the endives and cut them in half lengthwise. Cut in half again.

Choose a skillet large enough to accommodate all the endive pieces in a single layer. Add the oil to the skillet and sauté the onion, ham, and pancetta over medium heat. After a few minutes, add the mushroom slices and mix. Cook 3 to 4 minutes. Season with the salt and pepper and continue cooking until the liquid from the mushrooms has evaporated and the mushrooms turn golden. Add the endive pieces and mix well. Continue cooking for about 5 minutes, turning the endive pieces once. Serve on individual plates and sprinkle the top of the salad with chopped parsley.

SERVES 4

~ *Dolce di Limone Freddo* ~
Frozen Lemon Soufflé

1½ cups biscotti cookie crumbs
2 tablespoons powdered sugar
¼ cup melted butter
4 eggs, separated

Juice of 2 lemons
¾ cup sugar
1 cup whipping cream
Biscotti cookie crumbs, for garnish

Combine the cookie crumbs, powdered sugar, and melted butter and press the mixture into the bottom and 1 inch up the sides of a 8 by 8-inch glass baking dish.

Beat the egg yolks with ½ cup of the sugar in the top of a double boiler. Add the lemon juice and cook over hot water, stirring constantly, until the mixture coats the back of a spoon. Cool.

Beat the egg whites until soft peaks form, add the remaining ¼ cup of sugar, and beat until stiff. Fold into the cooled lemon mixture. Whip the cream until stiff and fold it in. Sprinkle some biscotti cookie crumbs over the top and place the lemon dessert in the freezer for at least 4 hours.

Remove from the freezer ½ hour before serving. Cut the lemon dessert in large squares, remove with a spatula, and serve on individual dishes.

SERVES 4

Una Cena per l'Innamorati
A Dinner for Lovers

Crostini di Salmone Affumicato
Toasted Bread with Smoked Salmon

Risotto con Asparagi, Pancetta, e Zafferano
Risotto with Asparagus, Pancetta, and Saffron

Scampi Saltati
Sautéed Shrimp

Insalata con Olive Nere
Salad with Black Olives

Fragole al Vino
Strawberries with Wine

Caffè
Coffee

SERVES 2

This is a dinner for two people in love, regardless of whether they are young, middle aged, or in their twilight years. It is a dinner to be shared along with past memories, present joys, and future dreams.

A smoked salmon paté on crusty French bread starts this special evening. A light Risotto with Asparagus accompanies succulent Sautéed Shrimp. The refreshing salad garnished with black olives provides a palate cleanser before a dessert of Strawberries with Wine.

Preparations

Some of the preparations for this dinner can be done ahead. However, this is also a good menu to prepare if you work. It can be quickly assembled within an hour's time.

If you desire, you can prepare the salmon mixture for the crostini in the morning and refrigerate it. Then assemble it just before serving so that the bread remains crispy.

You may prepare the risotto in the afternoon up to the point of adding the rice, and finish cooking it that evening. Prepare the lettuce for the salad and place it in the refrigerator. Shell and devein the shrimp and refrigerate them.

For your dessert to have the optimum flavor, make it in the morning so that the strawberries will absorb some of the wine. Then refrigerate it until ready to serve.

~ *Crostini di Salmone Affumicato* ~
Toasted Bread with Smoked Salmon

1 French baguette
4 ounces smoked salmon, chopped
1 tablespoon chopped onion
2 teaspoons capers, chopped
1 tablespoon chopped fresh parsley
3 tablespoons extra virgin olive oil

1 tablespoon orange juice
1 tablespoon lemon juice
¼ teaspoon freshly ground black
   pepper
2 parsley sprigs, for garnish
2 lemon slices, for garnish

Cut eight slices of the bread, place them on a baking sheet, and toast them under the broiler for few minutes on both sides, or until the bread is golden.

Mix the salmon and the rest of ingredients (except those for garnish) in a food processor until well blended. Spread some of the salmon mixture on each slice of bread and arrange 4 salmon crostini on each plate. Garnish with a parsley sprig and a slice of lemon.

SERVES 2

~ *Risotto con Asparagi, Pancetta e Zafferano* ~
Rice with Asparagus, Pancetta, and Saffron

2¼ cups chicken broth
½ pound fresh asparagus
4 tablespoons (½ stick) unsalted
   butter
1 carrot, finely chopped
1 celery stalk, finely chopped
1 medium onion, finely chopped
1 thick slice pancetta or bacon, cut
   in small cubes

1 cup Italian Arborio rice
½ cup dry white wine
¼ teaspoon saffron strands or
   1 envelope powdered saffron
½ cup freshly grated Parmesan
   cheese
Salt and freshly ground black
   pepper, to taste

Bring the chicken broth to a simmer in a saucepan.

Wash and trim the asparagus and cut into 1-inch pieces.

Melt 2 tablespoons of the butter in a medium saucepan over medium heat and add the carrot, celery, onion, and pancetta. Sauté for a few minutes. Then add the rice and let it brown for a few minutes. Add the wine and let it evaporate. Then add 2 cups of the simmering broth and the asparagus and mix well.

Bring the mixture to a boil, reduce the h[...]
ered, for 15 minutes. Mix in the remaining ¼ [...]
saffron, add it to the rice, and stir. Remove from[...]
remaining butter and the grated Parmesan chees[...]
with salt and pepper. Mix thoroughly and serve imm[...]

~ *Scampi Saltati* ~
Sautéed Shrimp

12 large shrimp, peeled and
   deveined
4 tablespoons olive oil
2 large cloves garlic, chopped fine
4 tablespoons chopped fresh parsley
2 scallions, white part only, finely
   chopped
½ cup dry white wine
Juice of ½ lemon
Salt and freshly ground black
   pepper, to taste

Rinse the shrimp under cold water and pat them dry with paper towels.

Heat the oil in a large sauté pan over medium heat. Add the garlic, parsley, and scallions and sauté for a few minutes; do not let the garlic brown. Add the shrimp and pour the wine and lemon juice over them. Let the wine evaporate over medium-high heat and sauté the shrimp for 3 to 4 minutes. Season with salt and pepper and remove the shrimp to a warm platter. Continue cooking the liquid, over high heat, until the sauce has thickened. Pour the sauce over the shrimp and serve immediately with sliced French bread to soak up the sauce.

SERVES 2

eat to low and cook, cov-
up hot broth with the
heat, and stir in the
. Season to taste
diately.

SERVES 2

e Nere ~
Olives

oon red wine vinegar
on salt
on freshly ground black
er
oons black olives with pits

glass serving bowl.
, and pepper in a small
Id the olives, and mix

plates.

SERVES 2

~ Fragole al Vino ~
Strawberries with Wine

1 pint basket fresh strawberries
1 tablespoon sugar

¾ cup red wine
Mint leaves, for garnish

Remove the hulls from the strawberries, rinse them in cold water, and pat them dry with paper towels. If the strawberries are large, cut them in thick slices, otherwise cut them in half.

Place the strawberries in a bowl, add the sugar and wine, and gently mix with a spoon. Refrigerate for at least 2 hours before serving. The longer the strawberries steep in the wine, the better the flavor. Serve the strawberries in tall stemmed glasses and garnish with mint leaves.

SERVES 2

Festa di San Valentino
A Valentine Feast

Manzo alla Milanese
Braised Beef Milan Style

Risotto con Porcini
Mushroom Risotto

Scaloppine di Vitello alla Marsala
Veal Scallops with Marsala Wine

Piselli con Cipolla e Prosciutto Cotto
Peas with Onion and Ham

Mousse di Cioccolato al Caffè
Chocolate-Coffee Mousse

Caffè
Coffee

SERVES 4

In America, from the time of childhood, Valentine's Day is a very special day. It is not only for lovers but for friends of all ages to acknowledge their friendship and love for each other. Cards and flowers are sent and received as tokens of esteem. The most celebrated of these tokens, however, is a heart-shaped box of chocolate candy. I, too, wanted to celebrate this special day with a special menu and to share it with some special friends.

I started the meal with an appetizer of braised beef combined with arugula, radicchio, and onion, topped with some olive oil and accompanied by crusty French bread. Mushroom Risotto and peas were the perfect companions to a classical Italian dish, Veal Scallops with Marsala Wine.

For dessert I chose a chocolate mousse, because chocolate is traditional at Valentine's Day. This light yet rich dessert was the finishing touch for my Valentine Feast.

Preparations

If you want to do some of the preparations ahead, you may prepare all the ingredients for the beef appetizer on the morning of the party and store them in the refrigerator until just before time to cook them.

Make part of the Mushroom Risotto in the early afternoon by sautéing the fresh mushrooms, porcini, and onion and then setting this aside until just before dinner. Then add the rice and finish cooking the risotto. You can also prepare the peas and onions in the afternoon. After you have added the peas to the saucepan, turn the heat off, cover it, and set it aside. That evening cook the peas and add the ham cubes.

The Veal Scallops, however, should be prepared that evening. They cook quickly and their flavor is best if served immediately after cooking.

If you like, you can make the dessert the day before the party and place it in the refrigerator.

~ *Manzo alla Milanese* ~
Braised Beef Milan Style

¾ *pound piece of top round of beef,*
    trimmed of any fat
½ *cup arugula, chopped coarsely*
½ *cup radicchio, chopped coarsely*
20 *thin slices red onion*

⅓ *cup extra virgin olive oil*
Juice of ½ lemon
Freshly ground black pepper, to
    taste

Freeze the beef for 2 hours or until the meat is firm but not frozen hard. With a sharp knife, cut it across the grain into very thin slices. Place the slices between two sheets of plastic wrap; with a rolling pin, roll the slices thin. However, do not roll them too thin or they will tear. Place the beef slices in the refrigerator and chill until ready to use.

Arrange the slices of beef flat, not overlapping, on a large oven-proof platter. Put the chopped arugula, radicchio, and onion slices on top of the beef slices. Place the platter in a preheated 450° oven for a few minutes. As soon as the beef turns pale, remove it from the oven.

Divide the beef slices, radicchio, arugula, and onion among 4 plates. Pour some of the oil and lemon juice over each serving and sprinkle with freshly grated black pepper. Serve immediately with sliced French bread.

SERVES 4

~ *Risotto con Porcini* ~
Mushroom Risotto

2 ounces dried porcini mushrooms
½ pound fresh mushrooms, sliced
3 tablespoons unsalted butter
2 tablespoons olive oil
1 small onion, finely chopped
2 cups Italian Arborio rice
3 cups chicken broth

½ teaspoon salt
¼ teaspoon freshly ground black
   pepper
½ cup freshly grated Parmesan
   cheese
2 tablespoons chopped fresh parsley

Soak the dried porcini in a small bowl in 1 cup of warm water for 15 minutes, then drain, rinse, and chop the mushrooms into small pieces. Reserve the soaking water, since it will be used later in the risotto.

Melt 2 tablespoons of the butter with the olive oil in a large saucepan and sauté the onion over medium heat. When the onion begins to turn golden, add the fresh mushrooms and continue cooking for a few minutes; then add the chopped porcini and stir to combine.

Add the rice and stir to coat the rice with the pan juices. Add the broth and 1 cup of water from the porcini and mix thoroughly. Bring to a boil, lower the heat, and cook, covered, for 15 minutes or until the rice is cooked but al dente. Remove the pan from the heat, season with salt and pepper, and stir in the remaining 1 tablespoon butter and the Parmesan cheese. Sprinkle fresh parsley on top of the rice and serve promptly.

SERVES 4

~ *Scaloppine di Vitello alla Marsala* ~
Veal Scallops with Marsala Wine

8 veal scallops (about 1 to 1¼ pounds)
Salt and freshly ground black pepper
⅓ cup flour
3 tablespoons unsalted butter

3 tablespoons olive oil
2 cloves garlic, peeled and cut in half
½ cup Marsala wine
1 tablespoon fresh chopped Italian parsley

Ask the butcher to cut the veal scallops across the grain from the top round. If cut this way, the veal will be very tender. However, if cut along the grain the veal scallops will shrivel and curl up while cooking. Place the scallops flat between two sheets of waxed paper and pound them gently until they are flattened. Season the veal pieces on both sides with salt and pepper, dip them in flour, and shake off the excess flour.

Melt 2 tablespoons of butter with the oil in a large frying pan over medium-high heat. When the butter begins to bubble, add the veal scallops and the garlic. Fry for 1 minute on each side over high heat. Remove the veal from the pan and keep warm on a serving dish. Discard the garlic.

Add the remaining tablespoon of butter to the pan, stir, and deglaze the pan with the Marsala wine. Reduce the heat to low and return the scallops to the pan, turning each one over once and basting it with the sauce. Transfer the veal to a warmed serving platter, pour the sauce over them, and sprinkle with fresh parsley. Serve immediately.

SERVES 4

~ *Piselli con Cipolla e Prosciutto Cotto* ~
Peas with Onion and Ham

2 tablespoons olive oil
2 tablespoons unsalted butter
1½ medium onions, finely chopped
1 (10 ounce) package frozen petite
    peas, thawed, or 2 cups shelled
    fresh petite peas

2 tablespoons chicken broth
1 4-ounce slice cooked ham, diced
½ teaspoon salt
¼ teaspoon freshly ground black
    pepper

Heat the oil and butter in a medium saucepan, add the onion, and sauté over medium heat until the onion is soft. Add the peas and the broth, stir and cook, covered, on low heat for 5 to 6 minutes. Uncover the saucepan, add the diced ham, season with the salt and pepper, mix well, and serve.

    If using the fresh petite peas, cook them only for 2 to 3 minutes.

SERVES 4

~ *Mousse di Cioccolato al Caffè* ~
Chocolate-Coffee Mousse

4 tablespoons strong coffee, prefer-
    ably espresso
4 ounces unsweetened chocolate

7 tablespoons sugar
4 eggs, separated

Combine the coffee, chocolate, and sugar in a small saucepan and melt over low heat, stirring constantly for about 4 minutes or until the chocolate is completely melted and the mixture is creamy and smooth. Remove from heat and add one egg yolk at a time, mixing well after each addition, until completely blended.

    Whip the egg whites until stiff. Fold them into the chocolate mixture a little at a time. Spoon the mousse into 4 stemmed glasses. Refrigerate at least 2 hours before serving.

SERVES 4

Festa di Mare
Seafood Feast

Cappe Sante Salmonate
Scallop Salmon Mousse

Tagliolini con Salsa di Scampi
Tagliolini with Shrimp Sauce

Salmone con Zucchine
Salmon with Zucchini

Mousse di Limone e Lamponi
Lemon-Raspberry Mousse

Caffè
Coffee

SERVES 6

Seafood has always been a great part of Italian cuisine, since Italy is surrounded on three sides by water — the Adriatic and Mediterranean Seas. The Italians have traditionally been known as fishermen, and the catch of the day frequently becomes the dish of the day.

In honor of this Italian aquatic heritage, I decided to design an all-seafood dinner. For an appetizer there is a baked salmon-scallop mousse. This is followed by a pasta with shrimp sauce. Salmon with Zucchini is the third seafood dish.

In the summer, particularly in northern Italy, berries of all types are used for dessert. Raspberries grow wild in the Alpine hills of the north and are commercially grown in the Lombardy and Piedmont regions. To incorporate the raspberries of my native area, I have chosen to conclude this Seafood Feast with a Lemon-Raspberry Mousse.

Preparations

Since this dinner is a quick one to prepare, you do not need to do a great deal of preparation ahead of time. However, the scallop-salmon mixture can be prepared a few hours ahead, placed in the scallop shells, and refrigerated until ready to go in the oven.

If you do want to prepare part of this meal ahead, you can make the shrimp sauce 1 hour before your guests are to arrive and remove it from the heat.

You can also do some advance preparation for the Salmon with Zucchini early in the afternoon. Cook the zucchini until barely al dente. You can also chop the herbs for this dish and slice the salmon, if not purchased already sliced. Place all of the ingredients in the refrigerator until ready to cook and assemble the dish. That evening, warm up the zucchini, place it in a shallow ovenproof casserole, add the salmon slices and the herbs, and bake as directed.

The lemon custard for the dessert may be prepared a day ahead, including the addition of the berries. However, you will want to whip part of the cream just before dinner so that it will be ready to garnish the desserts at serving time.

~ *Cappe Sante Salmonate* ~
Scallop Salmon Mousse

6 ounces coho salmon, skinless and boneless
½ cup whipping cream
½ teaspoon salt
½ teaspoon freshly ground black pepper
2 tablespoons olive oil

1 shallot, finely chopped
6 large sea scallops
1/3 cup dry vermouth
2 tablespoons bread crumbs
2 tablespoons chopped fresh parsley
6 ovenproof scallop shells, for baking

Remove any remaining fish bones from the salmon, chop coarsely, and place in the bowl of a food processor. Pulse at high speed for a few seconds, then add the cream, and blend to a creamy consistency. Season with ¼ teaspoon of the salt and ¼ teaspoon of the pepper. Divide the mixture among 6 ovenproof scallop shells.

Heat the olive oil in a skillet over medium-high heat and sauté the chopped shallot for 2 minutes. Add the scallops, and season with the remaining ¼ teaspoon of salt and the remaining ¼ teaspoon of pepper. Sauté over medium-high heat for a few minutes. Remove the scallops, add the vermouth, and let it evaporate over high heat until it is almost eliminated. Then place the scallops back into the skillet for few seconds to glaze them. Remove from heat.

Add a glazed scallop with some sauce to the top of each salmon mousse and sprinkle 1 tablespoon of bread crumbs over each scallop. Bake in a preheated 450° oven for 5 minutes or until the bread crumbs turn golden. Remove from the oven and place the shell on a small plate and serve immediately. (If available, place the shell on rock salt, which will keep the shell from moving.)

SERVES 6

~ *Tagliolini con Salsa di Scampi* ~
Tagliolini with Shrimp Sauce

1 pound medium shrimp
3 tablespoons olive oil
4 tablespoons (½ stick) unsalted butter
½ cup dry white wine
2 tablespoons brandy
3 cloves garlic, finely chopped
3 tablespoons chopped fresh parsley

Pinch of red pepper flakes
1 (14½ ounce) can Italian peeled tomatoes with juice, tomatoes finely chopped
¾ cup whipping cream
¼ teaspoon salt
¼ teaspoon freshly ground black pepper

Shell and devein the shrimp, rinse them under cold running water, and pat dry with paper towel.

Heat the olive oil and butter in a large skillet over medium heat. When the butter foams, add the shrimp, wine, and brandy and let the liquid evaporate over high heat. Cook for 2 minutes and then remove the shrimp and place them on a chopping board. Add the garlic, parsley, and red pepper flakes to the skillet and sauté over medium heat for about 2 minutes, without browning the garlic. Then add the chopped tomatoes with their juice and the cream. Mix thoroughly, bring to a boil, and cook over medium heat until the sauce has thickened slightly.

In the meantime, chop the shrimp, and when the sauce has thickened add them to the sauce along with the salt and pepper. Reduce the heat to a simmer and cook for a few minutes to blend the ingredients.

Cook tagliolini in boiling salted water until al dente and drain. Mix pasta with the sauce, place in a warm bowl, and serve immediately.

SERVES 6

~ *Salmone con Zucchine* ~
Salmon with Zucchini

1 pound small zucchini
6 tablespoons olive oil
2 shallots, finely chopped
½ teaspoon salt
¼ teaspoon freshly ground black pepper
1 pound fresh skinless salmon fillet,

thinly sliced
2 tablespoons chopped fresh seasonings to include 2 sprigs sage, 2 sprigs rosemary, 2 sprigs oregano and 2 sprigs thyme
Salt and freshly ground black pepper, to taste

Cut the zucchini in round, thin slices. Heat 2 tablespoons olive oil in a medium skillet over medium heat and sauté the shallots for 1 minute. Then add the zucchini, salt, and pepper and sauté for a few minutes until the zucchini is al dente. Arrange the zucchini slices flat in a large shallow ovenproof dish.

Place the salmon slices over the zucchini but do not overlap them. Sprinkle the fresh chopped herbs and some salt and pepper over the salmon. Pour the remaining 4 tablespoons of olive oil over the fish. Bake in a preheated 450° oven for 5 minutes or until the salmon is done. Remove from the oven and serve immediately.

SERVES 6

~ *Mousse di Limone e Lamponi* ~
Lemon-Raspberry Mousse

3 eggs
3 egg yolks
1 cup sugar
1 tablespoon finely grated lemon
    peel
½ cup fresh lemon juice

⅛ teaspoon salt
4 tablespoons (½ stick) unsalted
    butter, melted
1 cup whipping cream
2 cups fresh raspberries
Mint leaves, for garnish

Whisk together the whole eggs, the egg yolks, and the sugar in a medium saucepan until the mixture is thick and lemon colored, about 5 minutes. Whisk in the lemon peel, lemon juice, salt, and the melted butter.

Cook over medium heat, stirring constantly, until the custard is thick enough to coat the back of a spoon, 6 to 8 minutes. Do not let it boil. Cool the custard slightly, cover, and refrigerate until it is well chilled, about 1 hour. Beat ½ cup of the cream until stiff. Mix ¼ of the whipped cream into the cold lemon custard. Then fold in the remaining cream.

Reserve 18 of the raspberries to garnish the glasses of custard. Fold the remaining berries into the lemon mousse. Spoon the mousse into 6 individual wine glasses and refrigerate until serving time. Just before serving, whip the remaining ½ cup of cream. Place a large spoonful of whipped cream on top of each custard and garnish with 3 raspberries and a mint leaf.

SERVES 6

Il Ricevimento
Cocktail Party

Funghi Ripieni con Salsicce
Mushrooms Stuffed with Sausage

Funghi Ripieni con Gamberi
Mushrooms Stuffed with Shrimp

Crostini di Fegatini
Chicken Liver Crostini

Pagnotta di Pane con il Salmone
Loaf of Bread with Salmon Mousse

Bresaola Ripiena
Stuffed Bresaola

Crocchette di Riso
Rice Croquettes

Crocchette di Pollo e Funghi
Chicken and Mushroom Croquettes

Crocchette di Pesce
Fish Croquettes

Crostini Rustici
Rustic Crostini

Crostini con Pomodoro e Basilico
Crostini with Tomatoes and Basil

Crostini di Fagioli
Crostini with Beans

Crostini con Formaggio di Capra e Basilico
Crostini with Goat Cheese and Basil

Cocktail parties are rare in Italy. Invitations are primarily for lunch or for dinner. If an afternoon cocktail party is given in Italy for a special occasion, champagne, wine, and punch are served. Salatini (cocktail snacks) accompany the champagne or wine. Punch is usually served to the children. Hard liquor is not served for cocktails or before a dinner. It is usually served after a dinner as an aid to digestion.

I have chosen a few hors d'oeuvres that typically would be served as cocktail snacks in Northern Italy. Some are similar to the type of finger food served at American cocktail parties. Your selection of these cocktail snacks depends on the number of guests and the variety you wish to achieve.

Preparations

Many of these cocktail snacks can be prepared in advance of the party. You can make both of the stuffed mushroom canapés early in the morning and bake them just before serving. The chicken liver spread can be made days ahead and then simply spread on toasted French bread slices. The salmon loaf is best made several hours or a day before the party. All of the croquette recipes can be prepared ahead, some to the point of final cooking or baking.

However, the crostini (toasted French bread) should be prepared just before serving to preserve the crispness of the bread. Many of the spreads for the crostini can be made in advance. You will find that these canapés are very simple to make and not time consuming. The Crostini with Tomatoes and Basil can be completely made ahead and served at room temperature.

~ *Funghi Ripieni con Salsicce* ~
Mushrooms Stuffed with Sausage

2 pounds medium white mushrooms (28 to 32 mushrooms)
6 tablespoons olive oil
1 clove garlic, finely chopped
2 tablespoons chopped fresh parsley
¼ teaspoon chopped fresh fennel
leaves, or ⅛ teaspoon dried
fennel

2 mild Italian sausages, casings
removed, crumbled
¼ cup freshly grated Parmesan
cheese
½ teaspoon salt
¼ teaspoon freshly ground black
pepper
½ cup bread crumbs

Wash and dry the mushrooms with paper towels, but do not peel them. Remove the stems and finely chop them.

Heat 4 tablespoons of the oil in a large skillet and add the garlic, parsley, fennel, and the crumbled sausage. Sauté for 3 minutes over medium heat, breaking apart the sausage meat with a fork. Add the chopped mushroom stems and sauté for another 5 minutes, stirring often. Then add the cheese, salt, pepper, and bread crumbs; mix and continue cooking for a couple of minutes until well blended. Remove the sausage mixture from the heat and cool for 10 minutes.

Stuff the mushroom caps with the sausage mixture. Pour the remaining 2 tablespoons oil into a baking pan and arrange the mushrooms in it. Bake in a preheated 375° oven for 15 to 20 minutes. Serve hot.

HINT: This recipe can be prepared ahead of time. Stuff the mushrooms, refrigerate them, and bake just before serving.

SERVES 8

~ *Funghi Ripieni con Gamberi* ~
Mushrooms Stuffed with Shrimp

2 pounds medium white mushrooms (28 to 32 mushrooms)
6 tablespoons olive oil
2 cloves garlic, finely chopped
1 tablespoon finely chopped onion
2 tablespoons finely chopped fresh
 parsley
¼ teaspoon chopped fresh thyme

½ pound raw shrimp, shelled, deveined, and finely chopped
¼ cup dry white wine
½ teaspoon salt
¼ teaspoon freshly ground black
 pepper
¼ cup freshly grated Parmesan
 cheese
½ cup bread crumbs

Wash and dry the mushrooms with paper towels, but do not peel them. Remove the stems and finely chop them.

Heat 4 tablespoons of the oil in a large skillet and add the garlic, onion, parsley, thyme, chopped mushroom stems, and chopped shrimp. Sauté for 2 to 3 minutes over medium heat. Add the wine, salt, pepper, and cheese and sauté for another 5 minutes, stirring frequently. Then add the bread crumbs and mix until well blended. If all of the liquid has not evaporated, increase the heat and cook until it is gone. Cool the shrimp mixture 10 minutes and then stuff the mushroom caps.

Pour the remaining 2 tablespoons oil into a baking pan and place the mushrooms in it. Bake in a preheated 375° oven for 15 to 20 minutes. Serve hot.

HINT: This recipe can be prepared ahead of time. Stuff the mushrooms, refrigerate them, and bake before serving.

SERVES 8

~ *Crostini di Fegatini* ~
Chicken Liver Crostini

1 pound chicken livers
14 tablespoons (1¾ sticks) butter
1 large onion, chopped
2 cloves garlic, finely chopped
2 slices pancetta or lean bacon,
    diced
2 tablespoons chopped fresh parsley

1 cup dry white wine
¼ teaspoon salt
¼ teaspoon freshly ground black
    pepper
1 tablespoon capers, drained
2 teaspoons anchovy paste

Rinse the chicken livers under running water and pat them dry with paper towels.

Melt 3 tablespoons of the butter in a large skillet and when it starts to foam, add the onion, garlic, pancetta, and parsley. Sauté over medium heat until the onion is limp. Add the chicken livers and continue cooking for 20 minutes, stirring often.

Add the wine, salt, and pepper and cook until all of the wine has evaporated. Add the capers and anchovy paste, mix, and cook for 2 more minutes. Remove the liver mixture from the heat and let it cool. Place it in the bowl of a food processor and purée, adding the remaining 11 tablespoons of butter a few pieces at a time until well blended. Refrigerate until ready to serve.

To serve, spread the liver paté on slices of toasted French bread (crostini), or serve it in a bowl accompanied by slices of French bread.

HINT: The paté can be made a few days ahead and refrigerated.

SERVES 10 to 12

~ *Pagnotta di Pane con il Salmone* ~
Loaf of Bread with Salmon Mousse

1 (2 pound) loaf or 2 (1 pound)
    loaves white bread, unsliced
    (preferably day-old bread)
¾ pound smoked salmon
1¾ cups whipping cream
2 teaspoons finely chopped fresh
    fennel leaves or ¾ teaspoon dried
    fennel

¼ teaspoon freshly ground black
    pepper
1 (10 ounce) package frozen
    chopped spinach
1 pound cream cheese, preferably
    mascarpone (Italian cream
    cheese)
¼ cup finely chopped fresh parsley
Salt and pepper

Purchase day-old bread because it will be easier to cut and handle. Remove the crust from the bread, then cut it horizontally into 5 equal slices.

Place the salmon and cream in the bowl of a food processor and process until smooth. Add the chopped fennel and pepper and process to blend. Refrigerate the salmon mousse while cooking the spinach.

Boil the spinach and squeeze out all the liquid. Purée the spinach in the food processor, add half of the salmon mousse, and process until well blended, creamy, and thick. Refrigerate for half an hour.

Spread the plain salmon mousse on a slice of the bread, top with another slice of bread and spread it with the spinach mousse. Continue to add bread slices and alternate the mousses, ending with the fifth slice of bread with nothing on it.

Whip the cream cheese and parsley together and season with a little salt and pepper. Spread the cheese mixture over the loaf, covering the 2 sides and the top. Refrigerate the salmon loaf for 2 to 3 hours or until ready to serve. Slice and serve.

HINT: The salmon loaf can be made one or two days ahead.

SERVES 10

~ *Bresaola Ripiena* ~
Stuffed Bresaola

24 slices bresaola
12 ounces cream cheese
2 ounces Gorgonzola cheese

¼ cup chopped fresh parsley
Lettuce leaves, for garnish
1 lemon, sliced

Lay the bresaola slices flat on a board.

Mix the cream cheese, Gorgonzola, and parsley together in a bowl with a fork or electric mixer until well blended. Put the cheese mixture into a pastry bag with a ½-inch serrated tip. Place a line of cheese along the narrow side of each bresaola slice and roll it up like a miniature jellyroll. Repeat the procedure with the remaining slices.

Arrange the lettuce leaves on a serving platter, place the stuffed bresaola on it, and garnish with lemon slices.

HINT: This recipe can be made ahead of time and refrigerated.

SERVES 8

~ *Crocchette di Riso* ~
Rice Croquettes

3 tablespoons olive oil
¼ cup chopped onion
1 cup Italian Arborio rice
½ cup dry white wine
2 cups chicken or beef broth
5 tablespoons freshly grated
    Parmesan cheese
2 egg yolks
8 ounces white mushrooms, cleaned
    and finely chopped

1 shallot, chopped
¼ pound boiled ham, finely chopped
2 tablespoons chopped fresh parsley
¼ teaspoon salt
1/8 teaspoon nutmeg
¼ cup flour
2 eggs, beaten
½ to ¾ cup bread crumbs
1/3 to ½ cup olive oil for frying

To prepare the risotto, heat 1 tablespoon of the olive oil in a saucepan over medium heat. Add the onion and sauté until the onion is limp. Then add the rice and lightly brown it on high heat. Add the wine, let it evaporate; add the broth and bring the mixture to a boil. Cook, covered, on low heat for 15 minutes. Remove from the heat, add 3 tablespoons of the Parmesan cheese and the egg yolks, and mix thoroughly. Place the rice on a platter and spread it out to cool.

Place the mushrooms and shallots in a skillet with the remaining 2 tablespoons olive oil and sauté on medium-high heat for 3 to 4 minutes. Then add the ham, parsley, the 2 remaining tablespoons of Parmesan cheese, salt, and nutmeg and continue cooking for a few minutes until all of the liquid is absorbed. Remove from heat and let cool slightly.

Mix the cooled rice and mushroom mixture together in a bowl, and if the mixture is too wet, add some bread crumbs. Shape into round balls the size of a walnut and roll them lightly in the flour. Then put them in the beaten eggs, and roll in bread crumbs. Fry a few of the croquettes at a time, submerged in hot oil, until golden on all sides. Remove and place them on paper towels to drain. Serve warm.

HINT: The croquettes can be made a day ahead, then wrapped in foil and heated in a preheated 350° oven for 20 to 30 minutes.

42 to 48 CROQUETTES

~ *Crocchette di Pollo e Funghi* ~
Chicken and Mushroom Croquettes

Many times these croquettes are made in Italy with leftover chicken or beef, which was boiled, roasted, or barbecued. However, chicken is also boiled just to make this dish. For this recipe, boil 2 chicken breasts in 2 cups chicken broth to give the meat more flavor.

4 tablespoons unsalted butter
4 tablespoons flour
1½ cups milk
¼ teaspoon nutmeg
¼ cup freshly grated Parmesan
    cheese
2 tablespoons olive oil
4 ounces white mushrooms, cleaned
    and finely chopped
½ teaspoon finely chopped garlic

2 tablespoons chopped fresh parsley
¾ pound boiled chicken breasts,
    finely chopped
2 eggs, beaten
½ teaspoon salt
¼ teaspoon white pepper
1 cup bread crumbs
½ to 1 cup olive oil, for frying
1 lemon, cut in wedges

To make the white sauce for the croquettes, melt the butter in a saucepan over medium heat and blend in the flour. Add the milk, stirring constantly, bring to the boiling point, and cook over low heat for 10 minutes or until the sauce is very thick. Remove from heat, stir in the nutmeg and Parmesan cheese, and let the mixture cool.

Heat the 2 tablespoons olive oil in a skillet, add the mushrooms, garlic, and parsley, and sauté over medium heat for 3 to 4 minutes or until all the liquid is absorbed.

Mix the chicken, white sauce, sautéed mushrooms, eggs, salt, and pepper in a large bowl. Taste for seasoning, then chill the mixture in the refrigerator for 2 hours.

You can prepare the croquettes to this point up to one day ahead.

Shape the chicken mixture into small round croquettes, roll them in the bread crumbs, and fry them in hot olive oil until golden. As they are cooked, place them on a platter lined with paper towels to drain. Serve hot with lemon wedges.

HINT: You can also prepare these croquettes for a dinner. Instead of making small round croquettes, make large ones.

56 to 60 CROQUETTES

~ *Crocchette di Pesce* ~
Fish Croquettes

3 medium potatoes, peeled and
    quartered
3 tablespoons milk
1 egg
1 pound swordfish, halibut, or other
    firm fish
½ medium onion, cut into two
    equal pieces
1 bay leaf
1 lemon, cut in half
½ teaspoon salt

4 tablespoons (½ stick) unsalted
    butter, cut in pieces
¼ pound white mushrooms, finely
    chopped
2 ounces ham, finely chopped
1 clove garlic, finely chopped
2 tablespoons chopped fresh parsley
¼ cup flour
2 eggs, beaten
1¼ cups bread crumbs
½ to ¾ cup olive oil for frying

Boil the potatoes in water until done. Drain and mash them, add the milk, mix, and allow to dry out slightly over medium-low heat. Remove the mashed potatoes, place them in a bowl, add 1 egg, mix thoroughly, and set aside to cool.

Place the fish in a large skillet with enough water to barely cover it. Add the onion, bay leaf, and lemon, and bring to a boil. Cover and simmer until just cooked through, about 10 minutes. Transfer the fish to a chopping board using a slotted spatula. Remove the bones and skin from the fish, chop the fish finely, and place it in a bowl. Then add the pieces of butter, mushrooms, ham, garlic, and parsley and mix well. Add this mixture to the potato purée and mix thoroughly.

Shape the mixture into small balls and lightly roll in the flour. Then dip them in the beaten egg and roll them in the bread crumbs until completely coated.

Heat the oil in a large frying pan over medium-high heat, and when the oil is hot, add a few croquettes at a time and fry until golden on all sides. Place them on paper towels to absorb the oil and then serve them warm.

HINT: The croquettes can be made the day before up to the point of frying them.

45 CROQUETTES

~ Crostini Rustici ~
Rustic Crostini

2 tablespoons olive oil
1 large shallot, chopped
1 (10 ounce) package frozen
    chopped spinach, thawed
¼ pound boiled ham, chopped
¼ teaspoon salt
¼ teaspoon paprika

1 egg
1 cup whipping cream
1 tablespoon freshly grated Parme-
    san cheese
1 French baguette
⅓ cup freshly grated Emmenthal
    cheese

Heat the olive oil in a small skillet over medium heat. Add the shallot, spinach, and ham and sauté for 3 minutes. Then add salt and paprika, mix, and reduce the heat to low.

Beat the egg in a small bowl with the whipping cream and Parmesan cheese and add it to the spinach mixture. Mix well until the egg and cheese mixture is well blended with the spinach. Remove from heat and cool.

Cut the baguette into thin slices and toast in the oven on both sides until golden.

Spread the spinach mixture on the toasted bread slices, and place the grated Emmenthal cheese on top of each slice of bread. Place the slices on a cookie sheet.

Before serving, place the crostini under the broiler just long enough to melt the cheese and turn it golden. Serve immediately.

SERVES 8

~ Crostini con Pomodoro e Basilico ~
Crostini with Tomatoes and Basil

1 French baguette, sliced thin
3 to 4 large cloves garlic, peeled and
    cut in half
½ cup olive oil
18 fresh basil leaves, finely chopped

2 to 3 large ripe tomatoes (not over-
    ripe)
Salt and freshly ground black pepper
⅓ cup freshly grated Parmesan
    cheese

Place the slices of bread on a baking sheet and toast them on each side in a preheated 375° oven until golden. Rub both sides of each slice of bread with the garlic.

Warm the oil in a small saucepan with the chopped basil for 5 minutes on very low heat. Slice the tomatoes thinly and then cut again to fit the bread.

Arrange the pieces of toasted bread on a platter, pour some of the warm oil and basil mixture over each slice of bread, and top each with a piece of tomato. Season with salt and pepper to taste and sprinkle with Parmesan cheese. Serve immediately.

HINT: This recipe can be made ahead of time and served at room temperature, or you can refrigerate the crostini and warm them up under the broiler just before serving.

SERVES 8

~ Crostini di Fagioli ~
Crostini with Beans

1 French baguette
1 (15 ounce) can white cannellini
    beans, drained and mashed
2 teaspoons anchovy paste

1 tablespoon Worcestershire sauce
2 teaspoons Dijon mustard
1 tablespoon chopped fresh parsley
1 teaspoon olive oil

Slice the bread thinly, then place the slices flat on a baking sheet, and toast them in the oven until golden on each side.

Mix the cannellini beans, anchovy paste, Worcestershire sauce, mustard, parsley, and olive oil together until well blended and creamy. Spread some of the mixture over each toasted slice of bread and serve.

SERVES 8

~ Crostini con Formaggio di Capra e Basilico ~
Crostini with Goat Cheese and Basil

1 French baguette, cut in 24 ¼-inch thick slices
2 logs goat cheese, sliced thin
8 tablespoons extra virgin olive oil

4 tablespoons chopped fresh basil
Freshly ground black pepper, to taste
Lettuce leaves, for garnish

Arrange the baguette slices on a large baking sheet and place under the broiler and toast on one side.

Place a slice of goat cheese on the untoasted side of the bread. Add the oil to the chopped basil, season with pepper, and mix thoroughly until blended. Spread 1 teaspoon of the basil-oil mixture on top of the cheese on each slice of bread and place them flat on the baking sheet. Set aside.

Ten minutes before serving, preheat the broiler. Broil for a few minutes or until the cheese turns lightly brown. Cover a large serving platter with lettuce leaves. Arrange the crostini over the lettuce and serve immediately.

SERVES 8

Holiday Menus

Celebrazione Capo d'Anno
New Year's Day Celebration

Tradizione Pasquale
Easter Sunday Tradition

Festa del Tacchino
Thanksgiving Dinner

Natale alla Lombarda
Christmas Lombardy Style

Celebrazione Capo d'Anno
New Year's Day Celebration

Risotto con Porri e Prosciutto Cotto
Risotto with Leeks and Ham

Arrosto di Maiale con Salsa di Funghi
Roasted Pork with Mushroom Sauce

Fagioli Bianchi in Umido
White Beans with Tomatoes and Sage

Cime di Rapa Saltate
Sautéed Turnip Greens

Insalata di Finocchio e Arugula
Fennel and Arugula Salad

Gelato Affogato al Whiskey
Ice Cream Drowned in Whiskey

Caffè
Coffee

SERVES 8

New Year's Day is a day of celebration—the beginning of a new year; of new ideas; of hopes for better jobs, a better life, prosperity, and good health; and for making new promises or New Year's resolutions.

The Italians celebrate all major holidays for two days. The first day is to celebrate the event and the second is to recuperate from the celebration. The food that is traditionally served on New Year's Day varies with each region. In Northern Italy, it is customary to serve pork, beans, and lentils. Zampone or Cotechino, which are large pork sausages in the shape of a salami, are boiled and eaten on New Year's Day.

Since this type of sausage is almost impossible to find in this country, I have substituted a pork loin for the traditional sausages of this New Year's Day Celebration. I used ham in the risotto that starts the dinner. The pork loin is served with white beans cooked with tomatoes and sage. This is another traditional New Year's dish. Sautéed Turnip Greens complete the entrée.

A refreshing and tangy Fennel and Arugula Salad follows the main course. Since the dinner was a heavy and hearty one, I chose to end the New Year's Celebration with a light whiskey-ice cream dessert. In Italy, whiskey combined with ice cream is supposed to help you digest your food and leave you refreshed.

Preparations

Since this is a holiday you will want to spend as much time as possible with your family and guests. In order to do this you can prepare the sauce for the risotto early in the day and add the rice just before your guests arrive.

Prepare and season the roast with the herbs in the morning, cover it with foil, and refrigerate until an hour before cooking. You can make the mushroom sauce the day before, refrigerate it, and warm it up that evening.

You can also make the bean dish several days ahead. Cook your beans a little on the hard side, cool them, and then make the sauce. When the sauce has cooled, combine the beans and sauce but do not finish cooking the dish, just refrigerate it. Then finish cooking the beans the evening of your party. You can also prepare the turnip greens two or three days ahead. Boil the greens, drain them, shape them into balls, and then refrigerate. Cook them in oil and garlic that evening.

Clean the fennel and arugula for the salad that morning, place it in a bowl and refrigerate. Assemble the dessert when you are ready to serve it.

~ *Risotto con Porri e Prosciutto Cotto* ~
Risotto with Leeks and Ham

6 cups chicken broth
2 large or 3 medium leeks, white
    part only, chopped
6 tablespoons (¾ stick) unsalted
    butter
1 tablespoon olive oil
¼ pound ham, cut into small cubes

¼ teaspoon freshly ground black
    pepper
3 cups Italian Arborio rice
½ cup freshly grated Parmesan
    cheese
2 tablespoons chopped fresh parsley

Bring the broth to a gentle simmer in a medium saucepan.

Heat 4 tablespoons of the butter and the oil in another saucepan over medium heat. Add the leeks and sauté for a few minutes. Then add the ham, stir, and continue cooking until the leeks are soft. Add the pepper and the rice, stirring the rice to coat it with the pan juices. Gently pour in the simmering broth, stir a few times, and bring to a boil. Cook, covered, over low heat for 15 minutes or until the rice has absorbed the broth and is al dente. Remove the saucepan from the heat and add the remaining 2 tablespoons of butter and the cheese. Stir thoroughly. Transfer the risotto to a heated dish or serve on individual plates and sprinkle parsley over the top. Serve at once, passing more Parmesan cheese in a small bowl.

SERVES 8

~ *Arrosto di Maiale con Salsa di Funghi* ~
Roasted Pork Loin with Mushroom Sauce

2 2½ pound pork loins, tied
    together
5 cloves garlic, peeled
14 fresh sage leaves
4 fresh rosemary sprigs, about 4
    inches long

Peel of ½ lemon
1½ teaspoons salt
1½ teaspoons freshly ground black
    pepper
2 tablespoons olive oil
½ cup dry white wine

Place the tied pork loins on a board or a platter.

Cut each garlic clove into 4 to 5 pieces lengthwise. If the sage leaves are large, cut them in half. Remove the rosemary leaves from the stems, and cut the lemon peel in small, thin strips.

With a thin knife make about 10 cuts in the outside of the meat, about ½ inch deep. Fill the holes with a piece each of garlic and sage, some rosemary leaves, and some lemon peel. Also place some of each of the herbs and lemon peel between the 2 pieces of loin tied together. Sprinkle the outside surface of the meat with the salt, pepper, and any of the remaining spice mixture.

Put the olive oil in the bottom of a roasting pan and place the loin in it. Place the pan in a preheated 400° hot oven to brown both sides of the meat for about 20 minutes, turning the roast twice. Then reduce the oven temperature to 350° and roast the meat for about 25 minutes per pound. While cooking, turn the meat over four times. Pour the white wine over the meat during the last half hour of cooking. The roast should take about 2¼ hours to cook depending on the actual weight of meat. Pork is done when it registers 165° to 170° on a meat thermometer.

Remove the pan from the oven and transfer the loin with its drippings from the pan to a platter. Let the meat rest for about 10 minutes before cutting it into medium slices. Serve with the mushroom sauce.

SERVES 8

~ *Salsa di Funghi* ~
Mushroom Sauce

2 ounces dried porcini mushrooms
2 cups warm water
1 pound fresh mushrooms
1 medium onion, chopped
3 cloves garlic, chopped
2 tablespoons olive oil
2 tablespoons unsalted butter

½ cup dry white wine
1 (14½ ounce) can Italian peeled
    tomatoes, drained, tomatoes
    chopped
3 tablespoons chopped fresh parsley
½ teaspoon salt
¼ teaspoon freshly ground pepper

Soak the dried mushrooms in a bowl with the warm water for 20 minutes.

Clean the fresh mushrooms by wiping them with a wet towel, then cut them into slices.

Drain the porcini, reserving the soaking water, and rinse them under running water. Cut the porcini into pieces the size of the fresh mushrooms. Strain the mushroom water through a fine sieve and set it aside.

Heat the oil and butter in a large sauté pan, add the onion and garlic, and sauté over medium heat until the onions are soft. Add the fresh mushrooms and the porcini. Cook over medium-high heat for about 5 minutes, stirring to coat the mushrooms with the pan juices. Add the white wine and tomatoes and cook for a few more minutes.

Add the parsley, salt, pepper, and the porcini liquid and stir. When the liquid starts to boil, reduce the meat to medium-low and cook, uncovered, for 20 minutes, stirring often. The sauce is finished when all the mushrooms are soft but still a little firm to the bite. Serve the sauce hot over the sliced pork loin.

SERVES 8

~ *Fagioli Bianchi in Umido* ~
White Beans with Tomatoes and Sage

6 tablespoons extra virgin olive oil
8 fresh sage leaves
4 cloves garlic, peeled
1 (14½ ounce) can Italian peeled
    tomatoes, drained, tomatoes
    chopped
½ cup bean broth

Pinch of red pepper flakes
½ teaspoon salt
½ teaspoon freshly ground black
    pepper
6 cups boiled cannellini beans
    (recipe follows)

Heat 4 tablespoons of the olive oil in a large sauté pan with the sage leaves and garlic over medium heat, and sauté for 4 minutes, or until the aroma of garlic and sage permeates the air. Discard the garlic, add the chopped tomatoes, bean broth, red pepper flakes, salt, and pepper. Mix well and cook slowly for 10 minutes.

Then add beans to the sauté pan and cook slowly over medium-low heat until most of the liquid has been absorbed, about 10 minutes.

Pour the remaining 2 tablespoons of olive oil over the beans before serving.

FAGIOLI BIANCHI:
WHITE BEANS

1 pound dried cannellini beans
2 quarts salted cold water
6 fresh sage leaves
1 onion, quartered

1 celery stalk, cut in half
2 cloves garlic, peeled
1 tablespoon olive oil

Soak the dried cannellini beans in a large bowl of cold water overnight. The following morning rinse them in cold water and place them in a large stock pot with 2 quarts of lightly salted water. Add the fresh sage leaves, onion, celery, garlic, and olive oil. Bring to a boil, then lower the heat, and simmer slowly for 1 to 1½ hours or until the beans are just done. Reserve the bean broth for later use.

The beans may be served plain with olive oil, in a sauce, or as an accompaniment to sausages or pork.

SERVES 8

~ *Cime di Rapa Saltate* ~
Sautéed Turnip Greens

4 pounds turnip greens
4 cloves garlic, peeled and cut in half
6 tablespoons extra virgin olive oil

½ teaspoon salt
¼ teaspoon freshly ground black pepper

Trim the heavy stalks from the turnip greens, cut the light stalks and leaves into 1 inch thick slices, and rinse them under cold running water, then drain them.

In a large stock pot over high heat, bring cold salted water to a boil and add the turnip greens. Cook over medium heat for 15 to 20 minutes or until soft. Drain the greens in a colander, rinse with cold running water, and squeeze out the water with your hands.

Heat the olive oil in a large saucepan, add the garlic and sauté over moderate heat until golden. Add the greens to the saucepan, season with the salt and pepper, and mix thoroughly. Cook, uncovered, about 10 minutes, stirring occasionally. The greens are ready to serve when all the liquid has been absorbed. Discard the garlic and serve immediately.

Turnip greens are a good accompaniment to any kind of pork, especially turnip greens cooked together with Italian sausages.

SERVES 8

~ *Insalata di Finocchio e Arugula* ~
Fennel and Arugula Salad

4 large fennel bulbs
2 cups chopped arugula
5 tablespoons extra virgin olive oil
Juice of 1 large lemon

½ teaspoon salt
¼ teaspoon freshly ground black pepper

Remove the outside leaves of the fennel and cut off the stalks and feathery tops. Cut the fennel bulbs lengthwise into quarters, then slice them into very fine lengthwise slices.

Place the sliced fennel and chopped arugula in a large bowl. Combine the olive oil, lemon juice, salt, and pepper in a small bowl. Pour the dressing over the salad, toss thoroughly and serve on individual plates.

SERVES 8

~ *Gelato Affogato al Whiskey* ~
Ice Cream Drowned in Whiskey

Vanilla ice cream   *8 tablespoons whiskey (or more)*

Spoon ice cream into tall wine or parfait glasses and pour the whiskey over the top. The amount of ice cream depends on the size of glass or dish being used, and the amount of whiskey depends on each individual taste. Start with 1 tablespoon of whiskey and add more, if desired.

SERVES 8

Tradizione Pasquale
Easter Sunday Tradition

Risotto alle Zucchine
Risotto with Zucchini

Carrè d'Agnello Arrostito all'Erbe
Rack of Lamb with Roasted Herbs

Arrosto di Vitello con Patatine Arrostite
Roasted Veal with Small Potatoes

Soufflé di Carciofi
Artichoke Soufflé

Torta di Frutta e Noci con Zabaglione
Fruit and Nut Cake with Zabaglione Cream

Caffè
Coffee

SERVES 8

Easter is not only the renewal of religious faith, it is also the beginning of spring. It is the time of fresh herbs, new vegetables, and new tastes. It is also the time for spring lamb, a traditional entrée of Easter dinner.

My Easter dinner begins with a zucchini risotto and features two entrées—a roasted rack of lamb and a veal roast. If you choose to make only one entrée, you will need to increase the quantity. The artichoke soufflé is an interesting and tasty complement to either entrée.

A traditional Italian Easter cake with zabaglione cream ends this Easter celebration.

Preparations

There are several things you can do the day before Easter to prepare for the next day's dinner. Clean and cut the zucchini, and chop the pancetta, garlic, parsley, and onion and place them in the refrigerator in different plastic bags. Then make the risotto on the day of Easter.

Also on the day before Easter, prepare the roast of veal with the herbs and seasonings and then refrigerate it. Arrange bacon around the veal, then cover it with plastic wrap and refrigerate it. Make the basting sauce on the day before Easter and refrigerate it. Do not forget to remove the veal and the rack of lamb an hour before they are to go into the oven since they should be at room temperature.

You may wish to prepare the potatoes and artichokes on Easter morning. Place the potatoes in a pan with all the ingredients and set aside. You can also prepare the Artichoke Soufflé up to the point of placing the mixture in the oven.

The Easter cake can be made several days ahead, but the Zabaglione Cream has to be made at the last minute before serving dessert.

~ *Risotto alle Zucchine* ~
Risotto with Zucchini

6¼ cups beef or chicken broth
1½ pounds zucchini
6 tablespoons unsalted butter
2 tablespoons olive oil
4 slices pancetta or bacon, chopped
2 cloves garlic, peeled and cut in
    half

1 onion, chopped
4 sprigs fresh parsley, chopped
½ teaspoon salt
3 cups Italian Arborio rice
½ teaspoon freshly ground pepper
½ cup freshly grated Parmesan
    cheese

Bring the broth barely to a simmer in a saucepan.

Clean the zucchini and slice it thinly. Heat 4 tablespoons of the butter and the olive oil in a saucepan. Add the pancetta, garlic, and onion and sauté over medium heat until the onion is a light golden color. Discard the garlic and add the zucchini and parsley. Cook until the zucchini are tender but still a little hard.

Add the salt and then the rice, stirring to coat the rice grains with the cooking liquid. Then add the simmering broth and bring the mixture back to a boil. Reduce the heat to low and cook, covered, for 15 minutes until the rice is cooked through but still firm to the bite.

Remove the rice from the heat, and stir in the remaining 2 tablespoons of butter and the grated cheese. Mix thoroughly and serve on individual plates or from a warm platter.

SERVES 8

~ *Carrè d'Agnello all'Erbe* ~
Rack of Lamb with Roasted Herbs

2 racks of lamb, 8 ribs each
3 tablespoons extra virgin olive oil
1 teaspoon salt
2 cloves garlic, peeled
1 sprig fresh rosemary
1 bay leaf
3 sprigs fresh rosemary, leaves only
4 sprigs fresh thyme, leaves only
3 sprigs marjoram leaves

1 teaspoon fresh oregano leaves
3 cloves garlic
½ cup parsley leaves
10 fresh basil leaves
3 tablespoons bread crumbs
½ teaspoon salt
2 teaspoons freshly ground black
   pepper

Have the butcher prepare the racks of lamb by scraping away the thin strip of meat and fat between the bones, leaving the bones bare, so that when cooked, you can serve the lamb with little paper booties.

Brush the racks of lamb with 1 tablespoon of the olive oil and season them with the salt. Place the remaining 2 tablespoons of oil in a roasting pan and place the racks of lamb in it. Then put the 2 cloves of garlic, the 1 sprig of rosemary, and the bay leaf along the sides of the racks and place them in a preheated 400° oven. Turn the racks of lamb when they are browned, about 5 minutes on each side, then reduce the heat to 375° and cook for 20 to 25 minutes for medium-rare or another 5 minutes for greater doneness.

While the lamb is cooking, combine all the herbs in the bowl of a food processor and chop them. Then combine the herbs with the bread crumbs, salt, and pepper. Remove the racks of lamb from the oven, and cover the tops with the herb mixture, patting it down so that a crust will form. Return the lamb to the oven for 5 more minutes. Remove from the oven and cut into individual chops by cutting between the ribs. Place meat on a warm platter and dress the ribs with paper booties.

SERVES 8

~ *Arrosto di Vitello con Patatine Arrostite* ~
Roasted Veal with Small Potatoes

*1 (3½ to 4 pounds) veal leg roast,
boned, rolled, and tied or in a
net stocking
2 cloves garlic, peeled and cut in
slivers lengthwise
4 branches fresh sage, leaves only
1 teaspoon salt
1 teaspoon freshly ground black
pepper
4 slices bacon*

*3 tablespoons olive oil
2 tablespoons butter
2 slices pancetta or bacon, chopped
2 cloves garlic, peeled and chopped
coarsely
2 tablespoons chopped fresh sage
leaves
½ cup dry white wine
2 cups beef broth
½ teaspoon Worcestershire sauce*

With a small sharp knife, pierce the veal and in each cut insert slivers of garlic and pieces of sage. Sprinkle the veal roast with salt and pepper. Place the slices of bacon around and over the veal roast. Insert them in between the net or in between the strings, depending on the way the butcher has prepared the roast.

Make the sauce for basting the veal roast. Heat the olive oil in a saucepan over medium heat, add the pancetta or bacon, garlic, and sage, and sauté until the bacon and garlic begin to brown. Add the wine, broth, and Worcestershire sauce, mix, and continue cooking gently for 10 minutes over low heat.

Heat the 3 tablespoons olive oil and the 2 tablespoons butter in a large heavy ovenproof casserole or baking dish on high heat. Add the veal and brown it on all sides. Pour ¼ cup of the basting sauce over the meat and place it in a preheated 350° oven. Bake the veal 1½ to 2 hours or until tender. Turn the meat several times during cooking and keep basting it with the sauce. If the sauce looks too dry, add a little more water or wine.

When the veal is done, place it on a cutting board and cut into thick slices. Arrange the slices on a heated serving dish. Add a little water to the pan juices in the casserole and heat through to dissolve any meat particles attached to the bottom of the casserole. Taste and adjust sauce for seasoning, then spoon sauce over the veal slices and serve.

PATATINE ARROSTITE:
SMALL ROASTED POTATOES

4 tablespoons (½ stick) butter
4 tablespoons olive oil
16 small red potatoes, cleaned,
   unpeeled
2 sprigs fresh rosemary or
   2 teaspoons dried rosemary

4 cloves garlic, peeled
½ teaspoon paprika
1 teaspoon salt
½ teaspoon freshly ground black
   pepper

Melt the butter and oil in an ovenproof dish. Add the potatoes, sprigs of rosemary, and garlic cloves. Sprinkle the paprika, salt, and pepper over the top. Stir the ingredients together and place in a preheated 400° oven.

Immediately reduce the oven heat to 350°. Bake for 20 minutes and stir again. Continue baking for another 20 minutes. The potatoes should be cooked through and slightly crisp on top. If not, stir them again and bake them for another 10 minutes. Remove the garlic and fresh rosemary. Serve with the veal slices.

SERVES 8

~ *Soufflé di Carciofi* ~
Artichoke Soufflé

6 large artichokes
Juice of ½ lemon
4 tablespoons olive oil
2 cloves garlic, chopped

2 tablespoons chopped fresh parsley
1 cup canned beef broth diluted
   with ½ cup water
Béchamel sauce (recipe follows)

Wash the artichokes, trim the stalks, peel off all the tough outside leaves, cut off the tops, cut in half, and cut away the choke. Then cut the artichokes in wedges and into 1-inch pieces and put them in a bowl of water with the lemon juice for 10 minutes to prevent discoloration. Drain and pat dry with paper towel.

Heat the oil in a large saucepan on medium heat, add the artichokes, garlic, and parsley, and sauté for 5 minutes. Add the diluted beef broth, stir, cover, and cook slowly for 15 minutes. While the artichokes are cooking, prepare the sauce.

BESCIAMELLA SAUCE:
BECHAMEL (WHITE) SAUCE

4 cups milk
8 tablespoons (1 stick) butter
8 tablespoons flour
¼ teaspoon nutmeg
4 eggs, separated

1 cup freshly grated Parmesan
   cheese
1 teaspoon salt
½ teaspoon freshly ground black
   pepper

Bring the milk almost to a boil in a saucepan and set it aside. Melt the butter in another saucepan on medium heat, mix the flour with it, add the milk, and whisk until smooth. Add the nutmeg and continue stirring and cooking for 10 minutes. Remove the sauce from the heat and add 1 egg yolk at a time, mixing well after each addition. Then mix in the Parmesan cheese.

Drain the artichokes and add them to the sauce along with the salt and pepper, mixing very lightly. Whip the egg whites until stiff and gently fold them into the sauce.

Butter an 8-inch soufflé dish and gently pour the soufflé mixture into it. Place the soufflé in the middle of a preheated 400° oven for 35 minutes. Do not open the door until the cooking time has elapsed. When the soufflé has risen and is golden, it is ready. Serve hot.

SERVES 8

~ *Torta di Frutta e Noci con Zabaglione* ~
Fruit and Nut Cake with Zabaglione Cream

1 egg
2 egg yolks
1 cup granulated sugar
8 tablespoons (1 stick) butter,
   melted and cooled to lukewarm
1½ teaspoons grated lemon peel
1½ teaspoons grated orange peel
1 teaspoon anise seeds
1 teaspoon anise extract
1 tablespoon Grand Marnier
   liqueur

¼ cup pine nuts
¼ cup dark raisins
¼ cup light raisins
¼ cup mixed candied fruit, coarsely
   chopped (optional)
3 cups all-purpose flour, sifted
2 teaspoons baking powder
½ teaspoon salt
1 cup milk

Beat the egg, egg yolks, and sugar together until thick and pale yellow. Beat in the melted butter, then add the lemon peel, orange peel, anise seeds, anise extract, Grand Marnier, pine nuts, dark and light raisins, and candied fruit.

Sift together the flour, baking powder, and salt. Mix half of the flour mixture into the batter. Then stir in half the milk, add the remaining flour, and mix well. Add remaining milk and mix thoroughly.

Pour the batter into a greased and floured large Bundt pan or 10-inch tube pan. Bake in a preheated 350° oven for 50 to 60 minutes, or until a cake tester inserted in the center of the cake comes out clean. Cool the cake on a rack and then remove it from the pan. Serve wedges of the cake with hot Zabaglione Cream.

ZABAGLIONE CREAM:

8 egg yolks
½ cup sugar

Grated peel of ½ lemon
¾ cup Marsala

Beat the egg yolks and sugar in the top of a double boiler with a wire whisk until thick. Add the lemon peel and beat in the Marsala. Place over simmering water and beat vigorously until hot, foamy, and fluffy, for about 5 to 6 minutes. Spoon the hot zabaglione cream over a thick slice of the Easter cake. Serve immediately while it is hot.

SERVES 8 or more

Festa del Tacchino
Thanksgiving Dinner

Minestra di Zucca
Pumpkin Soup

Rotolo di Tacchino Arrosto
Roasted Turkey Roll

Puré di Patate
Mashed Potatoes

Piselli con la Pancetta
Peas with Pancetta

Torta con Grand Marnier
Grand Marnier Cake

Caffè Espresso
Espresso

SERVES 6

Thanksgiving is only an American holiday and is not celebrated in Italy. However, turkey is prepared in Italy in various ways. The Italian cooks do not roast the whole turkey. They separate the breast and cook it with or without a stuffing. The thighs can be stuffed, roasted, or cooked in different sauces. Pumpkin, another traditional food at Thanksgiving in America, is also used by the Italians. In Lombardy it is a risotto ingredient, and in the Milan area pumpkin is the basis of a soup with rice in it.

For my Italian version of a Thanksgiving dinner, I chose to begin the meal with a Pumpkin Soup. However, instead of rice, I added some pasta to it.

For the main course, I stuffed a breast of turkey with two different stuffings. Both of them are not only very tasty, they also make a colorful presentation when the turkey is sliced. The accompanying

Mashed Potatoes are enhanced with nutmeg and Parmesan cheese. The peas are flavored with pancetta to add another flavor dimension to the main course.

A Grand Marnier Cake gives a rich, tasty, and grandiose finish to the Thanksgiving dinner.

Preparations

To make the preparations for this holiday dinner easier, you can make the soup several days ahead and refrigerate it. Then add the pasta and cook that part of the soup just before serving it.

The two stuffings for the turkey breast can be made the day before and refrigerated. Then on Thanksgiving morning you can assemble the stuffed breast of turkey and refrigerate it until cooking time.

To give you some more free time when your guests arrive, you can prepare the Mashed Potatoes an hour ahead of dinner and keep them warm in a 300° oven. The peas also can be made one hour ahead and then reheated.

To further lighten the Thanksgiving dinner preparations, make the Grand Marnier Cake at least one day ahead to absorb the flavors of the glaze.

~ Minestra di Zucca ~
Pumpkin Soup

8 cups chicken broth
2 tablespoons olive oil
1 onion, finely chopped
1¼ pounds pumpkin or banana
   squash
4 ounces wide noodles

Salt
2 tablespoons unsalted butter
3 tablespoons freshly grated
   Parmesan cheese
2 tablespoons chopped fresh parsley

Bring the broth barely to a simmer in a large saucepan.

Heat the olive oil in another large saucepan over medium heat, add the chopped onion, and sauté until the onion is limp. Cut the pumpkin into strips and add them to the sautéed onion. Sauté the pumpkin strips, turning them often, for about 5 minutes.

Then add the hot broth, cover the saucepan, and cook, over medium heat, for about 50 minutes. Uncover, add the noodles, season with salt, and mix well. Cook the noodles for about 5 minutes or until al dente, over medium-low heat. Add the butter and Parmesan cheese and mix until blended. Just before serving add the chopped parsley, mix, and serve immediately.

SERVES 6

~ Rotolo di Tacchino Arrosto ~
Roasted Turkey Roll

1 whole turkey breast, 4½ to 5
   pounds, boned
½ pound ground pork
¼ pound Italian sausage, skins
   removed
1 (10 ounce) package chopped frozen
   spinach
3 slices white bread, crusts
   removed, soaked in ¼ cup milk
2 eggs
½ cup freshly grated Parmesan

   cheese
¼ teaspoon salt
¼ teaspoon freshly ground black
   pepper
¼ teaspoon nutmeg
2 tablespoons olive oil
2 teaspoons chopped fresh rosemary
1 cup dry white wine
2 tablespoons unsalted butter
2 tablespoons flour
1½ cups chicken broth

Have your butcher butterfly the turkey by slicing it lengthwise from the neck to the back, being careful to leave the meat in one piece. This will make the turkey breast twice as wide and half as thick. Remove any visible fat. With a mallet pound the meat until it is one slice of uniform thickness.

Mix the ground pork and sausage meat together. Cook and drain the spinach and chop it finely. Squeeze the moisture out of the bread and place it in a large bowl with the eggs, Parmesan cheese, salt, pepper, and nutmeg. Add the sausage mixture and mix thoroughly. Divide this stuffing in half. Add the chopped spinach to half of the stuffing and mix well.

Place half of the stuffing on one long side of the turkey slice and roll the meat over it just enough to cover the stuffing. Then place the spinach stuffing next to the other stuffing, separating the two by the meat. Roll the turkey slice over to cover both stuffings and tie with string or thread.

Place the turkey roll on a large piece of aluminum foil (shiny side inside), which has been brushed with the olive oil. Sprinkle the outside of the roll with salt, pepper and the chopped rosemary. Place the turkey roll in a baking dish and bake in a preheated 350° oven for 1 hour. While cooking, turn the roll over once. Then remove the aluminum foil, and pour half of the wine over the turkey. Return it to the oven for 10 to 15 minutes or until it is golden brown. Remove the turkey roll, set it aside, and keep it warm.

Melt the butter in a saucepan over medium heat and when melted, add the flour and mix the two together. Add the broth, mix, and cook over low heat for 5 minutes. Pour the rest of the wine into the baking pan, bring to a boil over high heat, and let the wine evaporate, while scraping up any residue from the bottom of the baking pan. Add the broth mixture, mix thoroughly, and cook over low heat for 5 minutes, or until the sauce has thickened. Pour the sauce in a sauce boat.

When ready to serve, slice the rolled turkey breast like a loaf and place on a serving platter. Serve with the sauce, the mashed potatoes, and the peas.

SERVES 6

~ *Puré di Patate* ~
Mashed Potatoes

2 pounds baking potatoes
1 onion
1½ teaspoons salt
½ cup milk

4 tablespoons (½ stick) unsalted
    butter
⅛ teaspoon nutmeg
¼ cup freshly grated Parmesan
    cheese

Peel the potatoes and onion and cut each into 1-inch pieces. Place them in a large saucepan with 1 teaspoon salt. Add water to cover and bring to a boil over high heat. Reduce heat to medium and boil until tender, 12 to 15 minutes. Drain thoroughly, return to the pan, and set aside for 5 minutes to let the water evaporate. Then mash the potatoes and onion with a hand masher or an electric mixer.

Warm the milk in a medium saucepan over moderate heat. Add the butter and let it melt, then add the remaining ½ teaspoon salt. Pour this mixture over the mashed potatoes, a little at a time, mixing constantly. Add the nutmeg and Parmesan cheese and continue mixing until well blended and smooth. Keep the potatoes warm for up to 1 hour in a 300° oven, until ready to serve.

SERVES 6

~ *Piselli con la Pancetta* ~
Peas with Pancetta

4 tablespoons unsalted butter
1 tablespoon olive oil
½ onion, finely chopped
2 slices pancetta, finely chopped

1 pound frozen petite peas, thawed
2 tablespoons hot water
½ teaspoon salt
¼ teaspoon freshly ground pepper

Place the butter and oil in a large skillet over medium heat. Add the chopped onion and pancetta and sauté until the onion is limp and the pancetta is slightly golden, but not crisp, about 5 minutes.

Add the thawed peas and 2 tablespoons hot water, mix, cover, and simmer for 5 minutes over low heat. Season with salt and pepper, and continue cooking, uncovered until peas are cooked, but not overdone.

Place the peas in a warm dish and serve with the sliced turkey and mashed potatoes.

SERVES 6

~ *Torta con Grand Marnier* ~
Grand Marnier Cake

1 cup butter, at room temperature
1 cup superfine sugar
3 egg yolks
1 tablespoon Grand Marnier
    liqueur
2 cups sifted flour
1 teaspoon baking powder
1 teaspoon baking soda

3 egg whites
1¼ cups sour cream
Grated peel of 1 orange
1 cup chopped walnuts
Glaze (recipe follows)
1 cup whipping cream whipped
    with 1 tablespoon Grand
    Marnier, for garnish

Cream the butter with the sugar in a large bowl. Add the egg yolks one at a time and beat well. Then add the Grand Marnier and beat until creamy, about 5 minutes.

Combine the flour, baking powder, and soda in a small bowl. Beat the egg whites until stiff peaks form.

Alternately add the sour cream and the flour to the egg yolk mixture, beating well after each addition. Then add the grated orange peel and the walnuts and mix. Fold in the beaten egg whites until blended.

Pour the batter into a buttered Bundt pan and place in a preheated 350° oven. Bake for 50 to 60 minutes or until a cake tester inserted in the center comes out clean. When the cake is done, remove it from the oven but do not remove it from the pan.

GLAZE:

1 cup fresh orange juice
½ cup sugar

4 tablespoons orange marmalade
⅓ cup Grand Marnier liqueur

Prepare the glaze while the cake is baking. Combine the orange juice and sugar in a small saucepan and bring to a boil over medium heat. Add the orange marmalade, let it melt, remove the saucepan from the heat, and add the Grand Marnier. Set the mixture aside and let it cool.

While the cake is hot, pour ½ cup of the glaze over it slowly. Let the cake absorb the glaze and cool for five minutes, then pour another ½ cup of glaze over it and let it become absorbed. Turn the cake pan upside down and place the cake on a serving platter. Slowly pour the remaining glaze on top of the cake and let it absorb.

Make this cake at least a day ahead. When ready to serve, slice the cake in large slices. Top with the liqueur-flavored whipped cream.

SERVES up to 12

Natale Alla Lombarda
Christmas Lombardy Style

Tortellini in Brodo
Tortellini in Broth

Bollito Misto
Mixed Boiled Meats

Cappone Ripieno Arrosto
Stuffed Roasted Capon

Patatine Arrostite alla Salvia
Potatoes Roasted with Sage

Monte Bianco
White Mountain

Caffè Espresso
Espresso

SERVES 12

Christmas is celebrated in grand style in Italy, with friends and family enjoying a large meal together. Christmas dinners, as well as other holiday meals, can last 3 to 4 hours with everyone enjoying the food and the camaraderie.

In the Lombardy region (Milan area), it is traditional to start the Christmas dinner with Tortellini in Broth. The Bollito Misto (boiled meats) that follow is also a very popular holiday dish in Italy. The broth of the boiled meats becomes the basis for the soup with tortellini. Thus the two are frequently served at the same dinner.

The boiled meats are usually served with a "mostarda di frutta" (mustard with fruits), and the best known of these mustards is "mostarda of Cremana." It consists of pieces of various candied fruits, which are covered with honey, wine, syrup, spices, and mustard. The taste is a delicious mixture of sweet and hot, rather then sweet and sour. Some of these "mostarda di frutta" are available in gourmet food shops and Italian delicatessens. If you cannot find this type of mustard, serve the boiled meats with the Green Sauce, or try some of both.

Capon is traditionally served as the main course at Christmas in Northern Italy. I chose to stuff the capon for this dinner and serve it with sage-flavored roasted potatoes. The recipe is for one capon to serve 6 and can easily be doubled. If capons are not available, substitute a large chicken.

The Monte Bianco, a traditional Christmas dessert, consists of a chestnut purée on top of a meringue. It may be served with slices of Panettone, the traditional Christmas bread. Since Panettone is rather difficult to make, it is usually purchased at the bakery or at specialty food stores. The dessert was named after one of the highest peaks in the Alps between Italy and France. Both nations claim the origin of this dessert.

Preparations

Although the boiled meats take 3 hours to cook, they can be prepared in the morning and set aside. Once the meats are added, the dish needs no further attention. To save work on Christmas Day, make the Green Sauce a day in advance and refrigerate it.

Once the boiled meats are cooked, you have the broth for the tortellini and need only to add them to the broth before dinner.

To have more free time on Christmas Day, you can make the stuffing for the capons a day ahead and refrigerate it. Then stuff the capons just before putting them in the oven. The potatoes can be cleaned in the afternoon, but they should not be cut until time to roast them.

The meringue for the Monte Bianco may be made the day before Christmas. Make the chestnut purée in the morning, place it in the refrigerator, and completely assemble the dessert an hour before dinner. In that way some of the moisture of the chestnut purée and the whipping cream is absorbed by the meringue. If desired, purchase a panettone to accompany the Monte Bianco.

~ *Tortellini in Brodo* ~
Tortellini in Broth

*10 cups meat broth (from mixed
    boiled meat, recipe follows)*
*1 (12 ounce) package fresh or frozen
    tortellini*

*1 cup freshly grated Parmesan
    cheese*

Bring the broth to a boil in a large saucepan. Add the tortellini, stir, and boil gently, over low heat, until the tortellini are tender but firm to the bite.

Serve immediately in individual soup bowls and sprinkle each serving with 1 tablespoon Parmesan cheese. Place a dish of additional Parmesan cheese on the table.

SERVES 12

~ *Bollito Misto* ~
Mixed Boiled Meats

2 large carrots, cut in 2-inch
    lengths
2 celery stalks, cut in 2-inch
    lengths
1 medium onion, peeled and cut in
    half
2 medium whole tomatoes, fresh or
    canned
6 sprigs fresh parsley, leaves only

2 medium potatoes, peeled
1 tablespoon salt
1 piece beef brisket, about 2 pounds,
    excess fat removed, rinsed
1 piece veal brisket, about 2 pounds,
    rinsed
1 chicken, about 2½ pounds, excess
    fat removed, rinsed
Green Sauce (recipe follows)

Place the carrots, celery, onion, tomatoes, parsley, potatoes, and salt in a large stockpot. Add 4 quarts of water and bring to a boil. Add the beef brisket and return to a boil. Reduce the heat to a slow simmer and cook slowly, uncovered, skimming off scum as it rises to the surface, for about 10 minutes. Cover the stockpot and simmer for 1 hour.

Add the veal and simmer for 1 hour longer, then add the chicken and continue simmering for 45 minutes to 1 hour. Do not overcook the meats.

When the meats are cooked, turn off the heat and leave the meats in the broth until serving time. They will retain their flavors better if left in a large piece in the broth. Remove the broth for the tortellini when needed.

When ready to serve, heat the boiled meats, remove them, and slice them. (Slice only the amount needed, since the leftovers will keep better in one piece.) Arrange the meats on a heated platter and spoon some broth over them. Serve with the Green Sauce on the side.

SALSA VERDE:
GREEN SAUCE

1 slice white bread
2 tablespoons red wine vinegar
1/3 cup finely chopped fresh Italian
    parsley, leaves only
1 tablespoon finely chopped fresh
    basil
2 medium cloves garlic, peeled,

    finely chopped
1 tablespoon capers, finely chopped
    (optional)
1 cup olive oil
Salt
Freshly ground black pepper, to
    taste

Remove the crust from the bread and place it in a small bowl. Spoon the vinegar over the bread and let it soak for 10 minutes; then squeeze the bread dry. Combine the bread, parsley, basil, garlic, and capers in a bowl and stir until mixed. Then add the oil in a slow stream, stirring constantly, until well mixed and the sauce has a creamy texture. Add the salt and pepper and mix again. Cover the sauce and place it in the refrigerator until ready to serve.

This sauce may be varied by adding 1 teaspoon of anchovy paste.

1½ cups of sauce—SERVES 12

~ *Cappone Ripieno Arrosto* ~
Stuffed Roasted Capon

1 4½ to 5 pound capon or large
    roasting chicken
Salt
1 carrot, finely chopped
2 celery stalks, finely chopped
1 clove garlic, finely chopped
½ medium onion, finely chopped
2 tablespoons finely chopped fresh
    parsley, finely chopped
4 tablespoons olive oil
1 tablespoon unsalted butter
4 slices white bread, crusts removed
½ cup milk

½ pound lean ground beef
½ pound ground pork
¼ pound ground veal
2 eggs, beaten
½ cup freshly grated Parmesan
    cheese
¼ teaspoon ground nutmeg
2 teaspoons salt
½ teaspoon freshly ground black
    pepper
2 sprigs fresh sage
2 sprigs fresh rosemary
1 cup dry white wine

Remove the insides of the capon, rinse it in cold water, and paper dry the inside and outside. Sprinkle salt inside the cavity.

Heat 3 tablespoons of the olive oil and the butter in a large skillet over medium-high heat. Add the chopped carrot, celery, garlic, onion, and parsley and sauté over medium heat until the onion is limp. Remove the skillet from heat and let cool. Soak the bread in milk in a small bowl.

Place the ground beef, pork, and veal in a large bowl. Add the beaten eggs, Parmesan cheese, nutmeg, 1 teaspoon of the salt, and ¼ teaspoon of the pepper. Squeeze the soaked bread and add to the meat along with the cooled sautéed vegetables. Mix all the ingredients with a large fork or with your hands until the mixture is smooth.

Place the stuffing inside the capon cavity. Close the opening with small poultry skewers, or sew it together with heavy-duty white sewing thread by overlapping the skin. Sprinkle the remaining teaspoon salt and the remaining ¼ teaspoon pepper over the capon and place in a ovenproof casserole or roasting pan. Spread the remaining tablespoon of olive oil over the capon and add the sage and rosemary to the pan.

Put the capon in a preheated 350° oven and immediately lower the temperature to 325°. Bake the capon for 2 to 2½ hours. (If you are using a large roasting chicken, bake it for 2 hours. If using two capons or chickens bake them about 30 minutes longer.) Turn the capon once or twice while cooking, adding the wine a little at a time and basting often with the pan juices.

When the capon is done, transfer it to a carving board. Remove almost all the fat from the casserole. Add 2 tablespoons water and cook over high heat, scraping up any residue that has stuck to the bottom of the pan. Cook for a few minutes to reduce the pan juices. Pour the sauce into a small sauceboat.

Remove the skewers or thread from capon, remove the stuffing and place it on a warm serving dish. Carve the capon and place the pieces on a preheated platter. When serving, pour a small amount of sauce over the stuffing and capon pieces. Serve with roasted potatoes.

NOTE: To serve 12, double this recipe and stuff 2 capons.

SERVES 6

~ *Patatine Arrostite alla Salvia* ~
Potatoes Roasted with Sage

4 pounds small red potatoes
¾ cup olive oil
12 fresh sage leaves

4 cloves garlic, peeled and left whole
2 teaspoons salt
½ teaspoon freshly ground black pepper

Scrub and dry the potatoes and cut them in half.

Place the olive oil and the potatoes in one layer in a large oven-proof casserole. Roll the potatoes in the oil until well coated. Add the sage leaves and the whole garlic cloves. Season with the salt. Place the casserole in a preheated 350° oven for 35 to 40 minutes, depending on the size of the potatoes. Stir the potatoes several times during cooking. Before serving, remove the garlic cloves and sage. Transfer the potatoes to a warm serving dish and serve with the roasted capon.

SERVES 12

~ *Monte Bianco* ~
White Mountain

MERINGUE:

4 egg whites
¼ teaspoon cream of tartar (if using
    stainless steel bowl)

1 cup superfine sugar
2 teaspoons cornstarch
2 teaspoons vinegar

Line a baking sheet with parchment paper and draw a 9-inch circle on the paper.

Beat the egg whites in a stainless steel or copper bowl until soft peaks form. (If using a stainless steel bowl, add the cream of tartar when the egg whites are foamy.) Beat in half of the sugar, a tablespoon at a time, beating well until the meringue is thick and glossy and stands in firm peaks. Combine the cornstarch with the remaining sugar and beat in a little at a time. Gently fold the vinegar into the meringue.

Carefully spoon the meringue into the circle drawn on the paper. Cover the base of the circle and pile the meringue 1½ inches high around the sides so that it will later hold the filling.

Bake in the center of a preheated 250° oven for 1½ to 1¾ hours or until the meringue is firm. Open the oven door and let the meringue cool on the baking sheet in the oven. Then completely cool and remove the paper.

CHESTNUT FILLING:

2¼ pounds chestnuts, shelled and
    skinned, see directions page 105
2¼ cups milk
¾ cup sugar
3 tablespoons dark rum

1 teaspoon vanilla extract
2 cups whipping cream
2 squares semisweet chocolate,
    shaved

Place the peeled chestnuts, milk, and sugar in a saucepan and cook over low heat, about 20 to 25 minutes, or until the chestnuts are very tender and have absorbed most of the liquid. Stir occasionally to prevent the mixture from sticking to the bottom of the pan.

Drain the chestnuts, reserving the liquid, and place them in the bowl of a food processor. Purée the chestnuts until smooth and place the purée in a bowl. Add the rum and vanilla and blend well. If the mixture is very stiff, add 1 or 2 tablespoons of the reserved liquid to lighten it.

To assemble the Monte Bianco, spoon the chestnut purée into the meringue shell, mounding it up to a peak in the center. Whip the cream until stiff and frost the chestnut part of the dessert with it. Sprinkle shaved chocolate $2/3$ of the way up the mountain. The Monte Bianco can be refrigerated for 1 to 1½ hours before serving. If desired, serve with slices of Panettone.

SERVES 12

Index